*Something
about Swans*

Something about Swans

ESSAYS BY

Madeleine Doran

THE UNIVERSITY OF WISCONSIN PRESS

The publishers wish to thank W. A. Weber
for his painting of the whistling swan
reproduced on the jacket and text pages of this book.

Published 1973

The University of Wisconsin Press
Box 1379, Madison, Wisconsin 53701

The University of Wisconsin Press, Ltd.
70 Great Russell Street, London

Copyright © 1973

First printing

Printed in the United States of America

For LC CIP information, see the colophon

ISBN 0-299-06170-1

For Ruth
if she were here

Foreword

These essays, of an old-fashioned kind once called "the familiar essay," have nearly all something to do with nature. But they are less accounts of things seen in it than reflections induced by the experience of seeing them. If they are for anybody but the author, they are hardly for dedicated bird-watchers or trained naturalists in their capacity as specialists. I am myself a duffer at bird-watching, though I have been casually watching birds (and other wild things) since long before the practice had become so common a pastime. I confuse one warbler with another, spring as well as fall; I sometimes commit the unpardonable sin of mistaking a vireo for a warbler; I think I see rare birds which cannot possibly be at the place I see them in; I miss seeing the common ones which should be there, and are. I accumulate as many questions as checks in my Peterson and Audubon guides. I am no good on a serious bird-walk because I am always being diverted by a flower, a tree, a stone, or a cloud. For the same reasons that I am not a good bird-watcher, I should not be a good scientist either. I should need to be both more patient and more accurate in observation.

But pleasure in nature is happily of more than one kind. It can come, as we all know, from just being thoughtlessly alive among wild things. Mere idleness, as Hudson has taught us in *Idle Days in Patagonia*, may be tonic, for it can refresh the deep wells of the spirit. More focused observation and reflection change the quality of the pleasure. One may observe in different ways according to one's talents, temperament, and tastes — for instance, in a scientist's measuring, classifying, and recording way, in a philosopher's generalizing, speculative way, in a poet's particularizing, affective, metaphoric way, in a painter's visual-izing, design-composing way. These modes of observing need not be mutually exclusive; the human mind is a far more varied and flexible instrument than our specializing age always remembers. Indeed, the power it has to specialize is com-plemented by the power it has to choose not to.

Another freedom it has is its ability to observe itself and its environment in a detached and "useless" way — that is, in a way not directed to a self-preserving end. It has a concomitant power to take off from a perception in any direction, to make imaginative or logical associations, to reflect, to speculate freely. Various sorts of perceptions act to free the mind in this way. Listening to music will do it for some, especially in a crowded concert hall, away from familiar surroundings and reminders of daily business; or walking alone on a noisy street; or sitting near the endlessly varied repetition of a running stream or breaking surf. The world of the creatures, animate or inanimate, all going about their business, or just being, independently of us, unnoticing, uncaring, seems to act as a special stimulus to loosen our minds from their bonds to daily chores and send them freely ranging. It invites them to play on the meanings of things, great and small.

These essays of mine, freely ranging and unspecialized, have been written over a period of several years. Some are based on a quick sketch set down immediately after the experience which started the reflection; some rely for facts primarily on my notebooks, records kept over many years of things noticed in my ramblings. All, whenever written, have been allowed to ripen and have undergone more or less revision. In all of the essays, therefore, whether old or recent, memory plays a rôle. As everyone knows, memory is a sifter, a shaper, a giver of form and emphasis. It may suppress, or even falsify, facts; it may alter the event it recalls, without the mind's being aware of the alteration, into something different from the immediate experience. But if one is less concerned with reporting what one saw than with reflecting on the seeing, one can hardly say that such recollections are "untrue." Their peculiar value often comes from the combination of memory and imagination, those twin creative powers.

When most of the essays were conceived, "ecology" was not yet a household word, and one could write about nature in an observant and reflective way without the ulterior end, the saving of the environment for future generations, which now informs much that is written on nature. Since I have little to say directly on pollution and ecology, I shall seem, I fear, very old-fashioned. But perhaps there is something to be said for being so. The possibility of being able to go on thinking in a relaxed and happy way about our experiences in the natural world is a not inconsiderable reason for seeking to preserve it.

Readers will notice that the essays have two very different

geographical centers. One center is in California and the far west, the country of my childhood and youth; I still count it as "home," as one usually does the place of one's family ties. The other is in Wisconsin, where I have spent the greater part of my professional life. The far west and the midwest are quite different worlds, each with its own riches for the observant eye and the listening ear. One is the geologically younger, grander, harsher world of rocky deserts, upthrust mountains, and sea; the other is the older, gentler, greener world of farm fields, lakes, and wooded hills.

The title essay, "Something about Swans," was read before the Madison Literary Club on 14 March 1966. It was written in memory of Ruth Wallerstein, who had been killed in an automobile accident in England in the spring of 1958. Since she had been a member of the Club and was known to most of the listeners that evening, the essay has a somewhat more personal tone than the others.

When I came to teach at the University of Wisconsin in 1935, Ruth Wallerstein was one of the University's three great ladies. The other two were Helen White and Julia Grace Wales. The three of them took me in and educated me with affection in the days of my young foolishness. Miss Wallerstein was elegant in person, exquisite in manner, finely strung, acutely intuitive; her scholarship was precise and deep; her ideas were passionately held. Her genius was very different from mine, but love has nothing to do with such distinctions. She gave me her wisdom in oblique and delicate hints, stood by me in times of need, shared with me her fine mind; and in herself she was to me a model of professional integrity and wisdom.

A Platonist and an admirer of Saint Augustine, Miss Wallerstein was naturally at home with Spenser, Donne, Shelley, and Yeats. She loved beauty, and she introduced me to my first wild swan on Lake Mendota. It is right that I dedicate to her memory these essays, the first fruits of the professorship estab-

lished by the Graduate School of the University of Wisconsin $\quad|\;xi$
to honor her name.

To Professor Robert Presson, Shakespearian and horticul-
turalist, my companion in birding and in many other things,
I gratefully acknowledge a special debt. I owe a great deal in
the essays to his informed and sensitive criticism.

MADELEINE DORAN
Ruth C. Wallerstein Professor
of English Literature

Madison, Wisconsin
March, 1973

Contents

Something about Swans

Something about Swans

If anyone wishes to find out everything there is to know, from anatomy to ecology, about the trumpeter swan, he may obtain from the U.S. Government Printing Office for a dollar a monograph entitled *The Trumpeter Swan*. In it there are two fascinating drawings of the tracheae of our two native North American swans, *Olor columbianus* and *O. buccinator*. *Olor columbianus*, the whistling swan, has a loop in its windpipe, adding several inches to the effective length of the air column with which it produces its notes. Now *Olor buccinator*, the trumpeter (more precisely named than its cousin), has an extra loop, coiled like a French horn inside the sternum; hence that much deeper pitch and greater resonance — rather like a bassoon compared to an oboe, except that the tones are not reedy. My concern will not be, however, with the loops in the windpipe, a subject in which I have no competence, but rather with the musical sounds that come out of it, or, more precisely, with the effect of these sounds on an observer; not with the mechanics of wing structure and of flight, but with the sight of those great wings in motion when a flock of a hundred whistlers rises into the sunlight. At any rate, the essay is about swans that I have seen, and also, to be truthful, nearly as much about ruby-crowned kinglets and water ouzels as it is about swans.

Let us begin with swans. This first story has to do with Ruth Wallerstein, whom older members of the Madison Literary Club remember with love. One day in mid-November in the early fifties, I noticed a whistling swan in University Bay, and I reported it to Ruth. It was the first I had ever seen, and I think (though I am not certain) that it was to be her first, too. Anyhow, she was aglow at my report, and sometime during the day we managed to dash off in her little car to see it. As we were making all haste across Observatory Hill, the chief of the campus police stopped us, and with no more tact or originality than were customary with him asked whether she thought she was going to a fire. She answered, with all her charm and a certain arch gaiety, that we were going to see the wild swan in the bay. If looks could kill, his would have finished her. His only reply was to write out a ticket. "You would think, wouldn't you," she said to me as we drove on, "that he could understand. I *do* think he behaved badly. It was most unreasonable of him." This story, so wonderfully characteristic of Ruth, delighted her colleagues and students, and they told it around Bascom Hall with merriment and affection. The actual swan in this anecdote has nearly disappeared from my memory, and you can see why. But the story is only a preface to the real discovery, for Ruth and for me, of whistling swans.

Several years later, in the spring of 1955, I had my first sight of the flocks of whistlers in their northward migration. Friends who told me about Goose Pond near Arlington, where swans were likely to stop, started me on that most happy adventure. On the second of April, and the first day in which the spring sun had some heat, a companion and I found Goose Pond, and found on it a small flock of swans, far off at the east end. The day might have ended there and been happy enough. But other birders at the pond told us to go beyond North Leeds to Mud Lake, a swampy hunting and fishing area lying in a valley between low hills. The search in the car took us quite a time, for our directions had not been very precise, and though we could see many geese and a few swans flying in and dropping somewhere behind a hill, we could at first find no road in. At length we found one going in from the north across a marsh and into an abandoned farmyard. Leaving the car and following the rather faint and occasional cries of swans, we walked half a mile or so across the stubble in a muddy cornfield towards a screen of poplars and a brushy hedge. We were not very hopeful of coming out where we would get any clear view of this hypothetical lake. But when we pushed through the hedge, there, a hundred yards away, was the lake in fact — or rather one end of it — narrow and shallow and still partly frozen; and there on it were the swans, a flock of twenty-five, some tipping up in the water, some standing about on the ice at odd angles, preening or sleeping — all in undress and at ease. Their talk, intermittent and casual, but always in those arresting musical tones, was like an orchestra tuning between numbers. Others, in twos and threes, came flying in, braking to light on the water, making thirty-six in all. They remained unaware of us, or indifferent, and we watched them for a long time. We had a sense of their temporariness, and hence of their rarity and preciousness for us, in their momentary pause between the two long legs of their flight from the Chesapeake to the Arctic. We went away with a sense of great fulfillment.

Now there was nothing in the least remarkable, outwardly, about this experience. It was, in fact, quite commonplace and not worth the telling unless one cares to speculate on why it is that human beings find satisfaction and wonder in such things; many of us seem to. What sets off a trivial event with such memorable singularity? In this experience it was not exactly the "firstness" of the swans that caused the pleasure. Every birder knows the pleasure of "firsts" — the first hooded merganser in a mixed flock of ducks, the first pectoral sandpiper among the waders, the first Connecticut warbler — or, if he is as poor as I am at catching birds in motion, even the first black and white or Tennessee warbler. This is a very real pleasure. It is a collector's pleasure or a hunter's: How many did we bag today? It is also, I am sure, Adam's pleasure, the pleasure of naming the animals. The early Biblical commentators all thought it most wonderful that Adam gave them all the right names the first time. To name is at the heart of all learning, the first step in mastery of the environment. But I am talking about something different and more complex, something in which "firstness" may or may not have a part. Why were these swans at Mud Lake exciting in a way those at Goose Pond had not been? The principal element of difference, I think, was in the "quest" — the search, the uncertainty of the outcome, the difficulties (very minor ones, to be sure), the quite unexpected intimacy of the sight, when reached. We were no Wilson and Cherry-Garrard searching in the Antarctic night for the emperor penguin colonies at the foot of Mt. Terror, or Kermit Roosevelt in the Himalayas on the trail of the giant panda. But we need not be. The difficulty and the achievement may be small, but it is the conformity of all parts to scale that counts. The figures in a marionette play seem life-size until the manipulator puts his head in among them at the end of the show. Our delight was as authentic as if it had been for a greater rarity.

This experience with the whistling swans had a sequel and a variant in Ruth Wallerstein's the following week, for when

I told her of the flock at Mud Lake, she insisted on being taken
to see it. It was on April 8, Good Friday, the first day of spring
vacation, and another glorious day, that we made our trip. I
had discovered the road along the south side of the marsh, the
one that runs along the top of the rise, from which one can
see the whole length of Mud Lake lying in the valley below.
I was fearful that the swans, whose business was to be off, would
not have stayed for us, but they had. In the distance we saw
them strung out in the water, a hundred or more, intensely
white in the sun. As we made our way down by a farmer's lane
and across the fields, their voices came to us in bursts on the
wind. The closer we got to the water, the farther they drifted
away from the shore. Yet we had a good view of them through
the binoculars, close enough to observe how the ferrous organic
compounds in the water in which they fed had soiled the romantic whiteness of their necks seen from a distance. Nevertheless,
their beauty held for Ruth: a beauty beyond speech. Only one
thing troubled her. She found their cries somehow discordant
— not, of course, discordant in themselves, but discordant to
the occasion. This response puzzled me at first, since their voices
were for me part of their special charm. Then the reason came
to me. These were for her Yeats's swans at Coole Park —

> Upon the brimming water among the stones
> Are nine-and-fifty swans —

the swans that

> Unwearied still, lover by lover,
> . . . paddle in the cold
> Companionable streams or climb the air;
> Their hearts have not grown old;
> Passion or conquest, wander where they will,
> Attend upon them still.

Yeats's swans were of course the mute variety, the *Cygnus olor*
of Europe.

Ruth's discovery, unlike mine the week before, came not as

the triumphant ending of a quest, but as the completion of meaning of a beloved poem; and necessarily, the poem entered into the meaning of the event. So, outward circumstance and inward state — a state prepared for by a myriad interconnections of temperament, experience, and memory — made for each of us, in our discovery of the whistlers, a new experience that was invested with special beauty, an experience in which the whole was something other than the sum of its parts.

In *The Tempest* there is a scene in which Ferdinand, fresh from the bewildering shipwreck, is drawn by Ariel's enchanting music to Prospero's cave.

> Where should this music be? I' th' air, or th' earth?
> It sounds no more; and sure it waits upon
> Some god o' th' island.

Miranda, whose experience of men is limited to her father and the monstrous Caliban, takes Ferdinand at first sight for a spirit, and when her father assures her he is mortal, she sighs,

> I might call him
> A thing divine; for nothing natural
> I ever saw so noble.

Ferdinand, with Ariel's strange music in his ears, looks up to see Miranda:

> Most sure, the goddess
> On whom these airs attend! Vouchsafe my pray'r
> May know if you remain upon this island,
> And that you will some good instruction give
> How I may bear me here. My prime request,
> Which I do last pronounce, is (O you wonder!)
> If you be maid or no?

All Prospero has done, by means of his magic, is to arrange the marvelous occasion; the rest takes care of itself, as he knew it would. "It goes on, I see, / As my soul prompts it," is his comment; "At the first sight / They have chang'd eyes."

Perhaps all I am saying, then, is that beauty lies in the eye of the beholder. I am not sure that I am wholly committed to this idea, but I shall not argue it or get myself into an epistemological bog I cannot get out of. Nor do I mean to be drawn into speculations on the so-called pathetic fallacy, though I was tempted. Perhaps one should call the sort of experience I have been talking about "poetic" to distinguish it from the more objective, detached, "scientific" kind of observation the human mind is capable of. I should like to suggest, however, that these two ways of looking at nature need not be at war with one another. The scientific view of nature and the poetic one, since they employ different modes of seeing, are not contradictory, one right and the other wrong. Each has its own validity. That they need not be mutually exclusive of one another, even within the same mind, is evidenced by the fact that many naturalists have been both scientists and poets. (Poets, of course, in the inclusive sense of articulate, literary men.) One thinks, to mention only a few, of Thoreau, Darwin, Muir, Hudson, Aldo Leopold, Rachel Carson — Audubon, too, though his poetry was more in his brush than in his pen. Indeed, the two gifts, the gift of patient and careful observation and the gift of interpreting experience, are so often joined in the same person that they may well be complementary. My own favorite, W. H. Hudson, certainly found no conflict in the two views. He thought of them as meaningless, the one without the other, as this passage from "Selborne," written in 1896, shows:

We are bound as much as ever to facts; we seek for them more and more diligently, knowing that to break from them is to be carried away by vain imaginations. All the same, facts in themselves are nothing to us: they are important only in their relations to other facts and things — to all things, and the essence of things, material and spiritual. We are not like children gathering painted shells and pebbles on a beach; but, whether we know it or not, are seeking after something beyond and above knowledge. . . . Intellectual curiosity, with the gratification of the individual for only purpose, has no place in this scheme of things as we conceive it. Heart and soul are with the brain in all investigation — a truth which some know in rare, beautiful intervals, and others never. . . .

It is Hudson, too, who best expresses what I have been talking about, in an account of a rainbow at sunset seen against the gray landscape of Patagonia and a stormy sky:

. . . after a time the westering sun began to shine through the rifts behind us, while before us on the wild flying clouds appeared a rainbow with hues so vivid that we shouted aloud with joy at the sight of such loveliness. For nearly an hour we rode with this vision of glory always before us; . . . while great flocks of upland geese continually rose up before us, with shrill whistlings mingled with solemn deep droning cries; and the arch of watery fire still lived, now fading as the flying wrack grew thinner and thinner, then, just when it seemed about to vanish, brightening once more to a new and more wonderful splendour, its arch ever widening to greater proportions as the sun sunk lower in the sky.

I do not suppose that the colours were really more vivid than in numberless other rainbows I have seen; it was, I think, the universal greyness of earth and heaven in the grey winter season, in a region where colour is so sparsely used by Nature, that made it seem so supremely beautiful, so that the sight of it affected us like wine. . . . But Nature is too wise

"To blunt the fine point of seldom pleasure."

The day of supernatural splendour and glory comes only after many days that are only natural, and of a neutral colour. It is watched and waited for, and when it comes is like a day of some great festival and rejoicing — the day when peace was made, when our love was returned, when a child was born to us. Such sights are like certain sounds that not only delight us with their pure and beautiful quality, but wake in us feelings that we cannot fathom nor analyze. They are familiar, yet stranger than the strangest things, with a beauty that is not of the earth, as if a loved friend, long dead, had unexpectedly looked back to us from heaven, transfigured.

These special occasions which, for whatever reason of circum-

stance, or association, or expectation, or rarity, or of many things
together, have for the person experiencing them some enhanced
meaning need not always be as deeply moving or as mysterious
as Hudson's rainbow. They need not be solemn; they may even
be comic. We may ourselves by a receptive frame of mind help
create them in the most unlikely circumstances.

I can illustrate from an incident or two that happened to me
in the Grand Teton National Park. In June of 1962, my mother
and I stayed for a few days at Jackson Lake Lodge in what is
quaintly known as a "cottage," fronting the marsh that lies
between the lodge and the lake. The "cottages" are a two-storied
row of motel-like apartments, furnished with every modern comfort, not excluding ice-buckets. In each a picture window frames
the bold and eminently photogenic shape of Mt. Moran. The
rates match the height of the peaks. The lodge itself was busier
than the campus at noon: a general hurly-burly of cars and
busses, of people on the move. Still, we tourists were only making a noisy fuss along the very edge of what we were there
for, not touching those great silent peaks beyond the lake. In
the cottage, I awoke towards morning in an impressive stillness.
The full moon was moving towards setting behind the Grand
Teton. Suddenly, and in an instant, the whole marsh burst into
clamor — every wild thing at once, as if on signal, calling out.
In the general racket I could distinguish many sounds, but few
certain — perhaps sandhill cranes, a coyote, a screech owl; certainly a great horned owl; and unmistakably, though I had never
heard them before, trumpeter swans. They demonstrated their
name. The clamor lasted for only a minute or two and then
every voice stopped at once; everything was as still as before.
I do not know how long I waited before the lightening of the
sky brought the more ordinary and dispersed stirrings of the
morning. This sudden pre-dawn awakening of wild creatures I
recognized from old experience with the San Diego zoo. Here
on Jackson Lake it was strangely thrilling, because it was an

authentic wilderness sound, one I was hardly entitled to hear, lying there as I was on my Simmons mattress. The voices of the swans were vouched for in the morning, for I could pick up in my binoculars six white dots on the edge of the lake a mile or more away. The next afternoon I walked out on a causeway I had spotted with the glasses, a causeway across a vast stretch of marsh and willows towards the lake. So far as I could see, no one ever ventured on it; everyone seemed content to have a browsing moose pointed out from the hotel terrace. But I ventured, not then knowing enough about moose to be frightened of them. Having gone a long way without any luck in seeing through the willow thicket, I was about to turn back when, at an opening where there was a little grassy meadow, I found myself facing — no, not a moose, but something much better — two elegant, red-capped sandhill cranes. They cried out at me, in their high, ratchety cry, they watched me anxiously while I got my camera into focus, but they did not fly. They merely stepped, slowly, and crying out, across the grass and into the willows. For me this was wilderness.

And so was the pair of trumpeter swans I came on in the Christian Ponds, while I was following a trail a mile behind the lodge. These *were* firsts for the eye, since one could hardly count those six dots on the lake. The pair was nesting on a beaver house; one bird floated out in the water five or six feet away, the other sat on the nest. I was above them on a hill, several hundred yards off, too far to disturb them. I saw her (or perhaps him) rise and arch her neck and delicately turn the eggs with her bill. The next day, on my return visit, the pair flew right above my head with all the tremendous stretch and power of their great wings. Of course they were, from that moment, *my* swans, passionately and forever. The next year I found them again in the same place, and this time I met a ranger with a dozen or so people in tow. I realized that this pair of trumpeters

was probably the most public and well-watched pair in the Park.
But I managed to laugh at myself and still keep my first memory
of them, with its sense of discovery, untarnished.

These experiences in the Tetons, one supposes, were not different in kind, but only in degree, and in the less exotic character
of the animals, from the experiences of those tourists who spend
a night in the Tree House outside Nairobi and watch the ele-
phants at the water hole beneath their feet.

The experience of true wilderness is beyond the reach of most
of us, and even the possibility of it will probably disappear before
very long for any man or woman. So one must make the most
of what is left. And somehow, by putting on blinders against
the encroachment of commercial man, and by looking resolutely
out to the wildness still there, one can still find it and know
it. Even wilderness may be as much a matter of vision as of
fact. For in 1843, when Audubon made his steamboat journey
up the Missouri to Fort Union in what is now North Dakota,
at a time when we should suppose the prairies to have been
still in their pristine bloom and freshness, he found them and
their life stale and unlovely. He did not see the "carpeted
prairies" or the "velvety distant landscapes" an earlier traveler
had led him to expect, but trampled ground, dead buffaloes,
and wretched Indians. In spite of the abundance of wild animals,
and in spite of the new birds Audubon found — the yellow-
headed blackbird, the western meadowlark, and the pipit he
named after his companion Sprague — he conveys little sense
in his account of being in wild country. The same wanton
destruction of bird and animal life he had observed ten years
earlier on the coast of Labrador, where the fur trade had reduced
the population of seals, foxes, martens, and caribou to precarious
levels, and where the "eggers" had taken an immense and bloody
toll, for eggs and feathers, of the seafowl on their nesting rocks.
So possibly, just possibly, in our far greater public consciousness
of the value of wilderness and wild things, and in the active

14 | desire of a few to save what we still have left, we are in a more hopeful state in 1965 than we should have had a right to be in 1843. But it is all very precarious. I have yet to tell the story of the water ouzels. They, too, have to do with wilderness, and also with "the fine point of seldom pleasure." In the Jackson Hole country in Wyoming, at a little ranch where I sometimes go — off the main road, at the head of a valley under the Gros Ventres Mountains, and on the edge of what is still mainly wilderness (I say mainly, for though there are no roads in, the hunters work it hard every fall) — in this country, there is discovery to be made every day: in the lodgepole pines by the cabins, Cassin's purple finches improvising — so teasingly like, yet unlike, the melodious eastern kind; down in the willows by the beaver pond, a calliope hummingbird buzzing in one's ear and displaying his shimmering gorget; above the fast water of the creek, an osprey hovering and chittering and dropping down for the hoped-for trout; up the draw behind the ranch-house an unregarded clump of calypso orchids; down the road a badger warily sunning her kits at the mouth of the den; on the trail up the canyon a bear's fresh pawmark firmly athwart the familiar deer and moose tracks; further afield, in the truly wild country, a herd of cow elk, fifty or sixty of them with their calves, streaming down a slope through the conifers; at home towards evening, the beaver feeding on the edge of his pond; at the salt-lick within sight of the dining-room windows a couple of does or a yearling moose or even a young bull with his season's "platters" half grown and in velvet; at sunset the coyotes yipping to each other all around the brim of the hills. The evening stillness belongs to the unhurried phrases of the hermit thrushes answering one another across the valley.

In this place of swift streams, there is a water ouzel's nest under every bridge. There is even, down near the mouth of the canyon, where Granite Creek flows into the Hoback, a famous ouzel nest on a granite boulder in mid-stream, visible from

the road. It is famous because Olaus J. Murie, a western naturalist we all know, wrote about it and made it a symbol of what
will be destroyed when the Army Engineers, in their unalterable
and relentless plan of damming every tributary in the Columbia
and Snake River watershed, build a dam across the Hoback and
send a lake up the lovely valley of Granite Creek. Murie's ouzel
nest is a very old one, but is still repaired and used every year.
I've seen the parents feeding the young, even seen their red
mouths gaping, not upwards like young robins, but downwards,
in an opening of the nest right above the racing water. How
the nestlings are secured inside is a puzzle to the human viewer.
But these were not my ouzels. My favorite one, up to now,
had been the one at Ouzel Falls in the Wild Basin in the Colorado
Rockies — where else should an ouzel be if not at his own falls?
I was to find my own at Granite Ranch. I knew there should
be one on Swift Creek, a small stream rushing down from the
peaks into the main stream in our valley. And one day, after
I had seen an ouzel dashing downstream, then upstream, I
worked along the creek as best I could over and around stones,
roots, and trunks; but I could not find the nest. I had given
up and was sitting, well-screened by fir boughs, at a bend where
the water, turning a corner around a jutting rock, raced and
roared as it came. Though I had no reason to expect him, the
ouzel appeared on the rock and started to sing — a free, caroling,
continuous song, piping and rolling, sometimes lost to my ear
in the noise of the water, then coming out strong, a song sung
against the roar and through it as if to sing it down, a wild
and wonderful song, and I should think not often heard by other
ears than an ouzel's. I took this exchange for the nest I never
found as an exchange with boot.

These memorable occasions, invested with some special
delight, are one sort of discovery. There is another sort, which
to this "seldom pleasure" has something else added.

In the fall of 1959 I was in Washington, working at the Folger

Shakespeare Library. I knew that whistling swans wintered on Chesapeake Bay, and I enlisted a willing friend to undertake a swan hunt with me. By inquiring around among knowledgeable Auduboners, we had heard that flocks might sometimes be seen around Kent Island, the eastern anchoring point of the Chesapeake Bay Bridge, and that on the island a good place to look was at Romancoke Ferry. It was a raw, windy November Saturday that we had to take for our hunt, and the whole expedition seemed unpropitious. A distant flock we noted as we neared the end of the bridge was of no use to us. We drove down the length of what seemed a completely deserted island, the old houses invisible in trees at the far end of long entrance roads, and the only house in sight a Charles Addams affair, abandoned and falling to ruin. We found the road to Romancoke Ferry, which hardly seemed a place when we reached it. The road ended at the beach facing the narrow strip of water between Kent Island and the Eastern Shore of mainland Maryland. Incredibly, to our eyes, but certainly, there before us, inshore, breasting the rough water and headed into the wind, rode sixty-nine swans. There were several cygnets among them, unexpectedly few — all that were left, evidently, of the spring brood. The wind was too cruel for us to stay long. And anyhow, what with the light on the moving water and the tears in our eyes from the wind, we could scarcely see through our glasses. So we found ourselves a place on the lee of the island to picnic in the car and listen to the sounds of another flock we could not get through the marsh to find. But we didn't care, having had our vision at Romancoke Ferry.

Why should I have been so deeply moved at the sight of this flock in the Chesapeake? For I was moved, intensely. These seemed to be — had to be, at that unreasoning moment — the very swans I had seen every spring at Goose Pond and Mud Lake, resting and talking, swans that had flown from those ponds to some unimaginable north country, perhaps Baffin Island, hatched and reared their young (with what losses!) and had now, under the strong annual compulsion by which their lives were governed, made, on their great sustaining wings, this long journey to the southern point of their orbit, the pivot on which they would once again, in late March or April, swing north. The whistling swans had been for me, until now, an adjunct of the Wisconsin April landscape. They were fixed to a time and place — a week on the calendar, a dot on the map — like the hepaticas pushing up from under the oak leaves to bloom beside Lake Mendota from the fifteenth to the twentieth of April, or like the warblers filling the Council Ring woods from the fifth to the twelfth of May. During the first week in April in Columbia County the swans had always entered my vision and left it. Now, meeting them at one end of their path, I knew (not theoretically, as I always had, but actually) that they moved in space and time, with a past and a future, and on a fairly fixed track that cut directly athwart my own limited vision. The huge envelope of space in which they moved north and south had its own limits, was one in which they lived their own lives from birth to death.

The excitement in this experience had something to do, then, with the pleasure recognition gives, us, but recognition of the familiar in an unfamiliar context. Recognition of the old in a new circumambience breaks the trite pattern, shakes the mind out of its complacency, invites a leap into new perception. This was a new kind of discovery, a new kind of knowledge.

I come to the ruby-crowned kinglet. Birds belong where one finds them. The first time I heard a kinglet sing was in mid-April at the west end of Ho-nee-um Pond in the Arboretum — to be precise, in the tangle of willow and red-osier dogwood that grows between the pond and the marsh. From a dogwood bush came a loud and melodious burst of song, delightful in its novelty; it was repeated often, with no very long pause between bursts. When I found the source of it, a four-inch kinglet, I was astonished and amused. After that, of course, I heard the song and a variant of it all about the path and in the crabs and hawthorns.

The point about the first hearing was that the spring day, the open pond, the budding willows and dogwood were adjuncts to the song, or, conversely, the song was an adjunct to them, part of a texture from which the separate threads could not be drawn without destroying the whole pattern. But kinglets do sing in other places. One bright day in mid-June, at about 10,000 feet up in the Colorado Rockies, I was rounding a corner on the trail from Nymph to Dream Lake, when from a fir tree at my elbow was flung out a song, loud, with a shaped melody, and several times repeated. I stopped, frozen, with an acute feeling, both delightful and painful, that here was a song I had heard before; but nothing about me — the mountain shoulder strewn with tumbled rocks, the clear thin air, the steep trail, the clumps of Engelmann spruce and alpine fir — helped me to place it. The painful urgency to fix that sound in a place and time, to fetch up the identity of it from the depths of memory, was like the urgency one has when awakening from a dream and feels it slipping into oblivion, to stop it, hold it, fix it, until one can take a remembering look at the strange country one was in just now. Happily, on that occasion on the trail, the memory came to free me. I knew I was hearing a ruby-crowned kinglet, and with the relief came a quite irrational delight. This was new knowledge — something vouched for with my own nervous system, not at all like reading in a book that kinglets nest in conifers in the transition and Hudsonian zones in northern latitudes or at high elevations. In breaking out of the pattern woven on an April day at Ho-nee-um Pond, kinglets, in my experience, had leaped from there to here, from then to now, and might leap into some unimaginable future.

One might illustrate this stab of recognition, both disturbing and pleasurable, from many remembered occasions, such as see-

ing a yellow warbler, that one knows in May in the shrubbery
on Observatory Hill, dart after midges in the seaweed on a
granite rock thrusting into the Atlantic spray; or hearing the
bodiless voice of the hermit thrush one thought belonged to
the deep oak woods beyond Pine Bluff on May evenings, flute
from the pines at dusk across a mountain valley in Wyoming.
I may say that this kind of magic will not work with mallards,
robins, grackles, or warbling vireos, those adaptable birds of
here and everywhere that have lost identity of place and so have,
for us, forfeited the pleasure of recognition to the pleasure of
reassurance.

The kinglet in the fir tree, the warbler in the Atlantic spray,
the thrush in the mountains have an affinity, I believe, with
the recognition that lies at the heart of one's pleasure in poetry,
a recognition that is at once a memory and a discovery, when
we say, at some passage in Virgil or Shakespeare or Tolstoy,
"Yes, this is the way it is."

Ruth Wallerstein died in England at the end of March in 1958.
Several years later, on one of my usual spring trips to Arlington
and Lowville in quest of whistling swans, I thought of that first
spring in 1955 when they were such a wonder to her, and I
wrote some verses about that day. If I may, I shall make of
them a period to this essay. They are called, after the day, "Good
Friday, 1955."

> The winter browns were there, and the chill wind,
> No apparent spring in grass or tree,
> But down below the hill in the long marsh
> The sun caught the life of open water;
> And there, fulfilling faith, they were, the swans —
> Not tentative in twos and threes, hinting
> Their return, but manifest in whiteness
> A hundred on the stream. For her this beauty
> Was epiphany. We crossed the stubble,

Tried for nearness, and their high talking
Came to us on the wind. The sound is wrong,
She said, thinking of Coole. But then they rose
In lovely clamor, many-voiced, a fugue
Of white and shadowed wings.

                                Now in the seventh year
The marsh has shrunk and roughened; this year's ice
Invites no guests; her voice, too, is gone.
Still, certain of north, on bowed wings
The companies come, reaching with stretched necks
For every farmer's pond; their resonant horns
Making a joyful noise.

The
Pleasures of Seconds

We all know the pleasures of "firsts" — the first skylark caroling unseen above an English meadow, confirming the poets; the first pair of trumpeter swans brooding atop a beaver's old house in a mountain pond; the first sight of some stretch of southwest desert in spring bloom; the first calypso orchid at the edge of pines on a Rocky Mountain slope. This pleasure of "firsts" is just as open to the apprentice bird-watcher consciously seeing his first rose-breasted grosbeak as to the marine biologist finding in a Pacific tide-pool a rare alga or sponge for the first time in his experience, or to the archaeologist unearthing his first Sumerian potsherd. |21

There is no doubt a difference of quality in these pleasures. The experience must be subtler, we suppose, for the scientist finding a rare first than for the beginner in observation, subtler still if the first is the first not just for him but for the world. Think of the richness of Darwin's days off the *Beagle*! It is hardly to be imagined. Yet discovery is the common quality of all these firsts, however they may vary in length and complexity with person and circumstance. Because our expectations are usually adjusted to our competence, the least ambitious of us can have the pleasure of discovery in a modest way. For us as for the scientist the first thing happens only once. The experience cannot be had again, whether the thing discovered be of the most commonplace sort or of the greatest rarity — the first myrtle warbler a novice bird-watcher sees and knows to be one, or the first Kirtland's warbler an ornithologist observes for himself in the lower peninsula of Michigan. Whatever the discovery, its uniqueness is an essential part of the experience.

Yet there are many accidental variables, apart from those already suggested, in the experience of "firstness." One of these is the difference between discovery at the end of a search when one feels that effort is rewarded, and discovery unexpected, when one just turns a corner and there the thing is. After something longed for is found, one would not forego the ardors of the hunt. In memory these are often the most treasured part of the discovery, conferring on the experience a value beyond the interest or beauty or worth of the thing discovered. The Seven Cities of Cibola as they truly are, not as they were dreamed to be, lie at the end of many a search; yet what Coronado who has survived the disillusion does not tell of the journey ever after, and polish in the retelling, to hearers willing and unwilling?

But discovery unprepared for gives the purer pleasure. One Sunday afternoon in May, in Madison's warbler week, I sat on my back porch writing. I had been across the street to the University Arboretum earlier in the morning, and had ticked

off my share of familiar warblers. I was content. But while I
sat searching for a phrase I happened to glance up at the leafing
elm, and there, in plain view on a low branch and busily feeding,
was a male prothonotary warbler. Although I had never before
seen one, as a Petersonian I knew at once what it was. A knot
tightened in my solar plexus and a radiating thrill went through
me. Insects seemed plentiful on the garage roof beneath the
tree, and the visitor stayed about in open view for a good while.
Word of its presence in the neighborhood had evidently got
about, for other Auduboners came looking for it after it had
left my tree; they went disappointed away, their searching
unrewarded. I had done nothing at all that morning to deserve
that lovely bird. I had sat idle while others labored. Surely we
are saved by grace, not merit. If I had not already inclined rather
to Augustine than to Aquinas, I should have changed my
allegiance that morning. Place is another variable. In fact, context is so important that one wonders if in our memory of a
discovery place (with its adjunct of time) is ever detachable from
the experience. I remember the first bald eagle I ever saw in
the wild as a great somber mark on a leafless cottonwood beside
the half-frozen Wisconsin River; only the dark current between
the ice was moving, and half a dozen crows, like yapping dogs,
cawing and flying about and baiting the solemn, immobile
creature. I remember my first coming on hepaticas in bloom,
in mid-April, in a still wintry oak wood, cold with the northwest
wind off the lake. The flowers made no show, yet little by little
revealed themselves in hundreds, in small clusters of pink or
lavender blooms rising between brown leaves at the foot of the
dark trunks. The troubled sky and the gray limestone ridges
running out into the Atlantic are for me a part of the look of
Irish heather and gorse in bloom. The song of the white-crowned
sparrow belongs to the place of my first heeding it — to the
pale sand and the dark green creosote bushes, bursting with
yellow bloom, of the Colorado Desert. Yet I have heard the

song often elsewhere, in willow thickets by mountain creeks in Wyoming, on foggy sea-cliffs in Oregon, even in our own garden in San Diego. Place and time are especially important if the discovery is of something within, not without; an affair of the emotions, not of things. We are apt to forget, indeed, so precious a memory the setting may be, that we cannot repeat the experience by returning to the place. We cannot have again the first kiss in the moonlight beside a shimmering lake. An epiphany cannot, by its nature, be repeated. If we should be moved to build a fane on the spot where we had the vision, we should do it for a memorial, a place in which to celebrate the event in decent ceremony; we should not, in wisdom, expect to see the goddess again.

All the same, we do go back to places of discovery; we do see things the second time, the third and fourth times, times beyond count. Indeed, we must see things again, must return to many places; if we did not, we should have neither knowledge nor history, should not now be civilized men, perhaps not men at all. There are uses and pleasures in "seconds," and in returns, as well as in "firsts." The pleasures may be quite as rewarding, only different in kind. It is about these rewards of seconds — less regarded, perhaps, than those of firsts — that I would speak. They are the Marthas of experience, rather than the Marys. We have need of wonder at times, but we cannot live on it. Our staple of experience must be things that recur, so that we can recognize them and give them names and go about our business without having to be surprised at everything. We need reassurance that a thing once seen may be seen again, that the world we live in is stable enough for us to feel at home in.

When we have seen the prothonotary a second time, we do not lose the first experience of it. Although we cannot have again the original surprise and joy (those we keep in memory to take on a rosy glow with time), we may have another thrill at seeing

so lovely a bird again, and a self-congratulatory pleasure in recognizing it. A better illustration, however, than the prothonotary,
which is too distinctive for recognition of it on its return to merit
a prize, would be a second sight of a more common warbler,
or of some hawk or sandpiper. If we recognize our bird as a
Nashville warbler, or as a sharp-shinned hawk, or as a pectoral
sandpiper, we have learned our lesson well. Then we experience
a comfortable, proprietary feeling that the bird is in some way
ours. We have added one to the number of species which have
emerged, with shape, color, and name, from the circumambience of things (differentiated in our minds by kind, but only
partially by species and individuals) in which we habitually walk.

Recognition often repeated takes on a different quality. Suppose we make another substitution — for the warbler or hawk
or sandpiper something more commonplace, say a goldfinch, a
cardinal, a robin, the birds we do not even remember seeing,
or knowing the names of, for the first time. The easy familiarity
we have acquired with such birds enables us to recognize them
distantly by some distinguishing movement or attitude or flash
of color, merely glimpsed in the tail of the eye. It gives us
assurance, sometimes even pleasure, not to have to stop and
heed the thing, but merely to note it in passing at an expected
place or time: "Yes, there you are." Our world grows ever richer
with the extension of this easy mastery to less and less commonplace things, whether they be in the mineral, vegetable, or animal kingdom.

An interesting consequence of this habitual, non-regarded recognition, is that if we catch a glimpse of something familiar *not*
at the right time or place we are instantly arrested, aware of
a disturbance, a wrinkle in the smooth surface of our expect-
ancies. Why, for instance, at dusk one August evening in a
sea-side park in southern California did a large bird with the
shape and shading of a bittern suddenly appear, flying up into
the branches of a Norfolk pine? It simply ought not to have

been there. Even if it were, possibly, an immature black-crowned night heron, it had no business being *there*, beside cliffs, rocks, and surf, very far from a marsh. But it *was* there. Why were half a dozen white pelicans (probably heading for the Gulf from their nesting lakes in Manitoba) afloat one morning on a small lake in Madison, far to the east of their normal course? Such anomalies invite us to ask questions and therefore to seek answers.

Most of us, with things not in our special line of interest, are probably content with mere name-calling, which gives us a comfortable sense of being at home with things in the landscape. And with that there is nothing to be ashamed of. But of course we may choose to go beyond bare recognition of our warbler or hawk or sandpiper. If we are curious enough and industrious enough, and if circumstances allow us to, we may find out second-hand, perhaps even first-hand, about its habitat, its food, its nest, its family life, with no clear stopping place. Such inquiry, done first-hand and methodically, is the way of the scientist and needs no elaboration or illustration. In it, recognition and discovery are reciprocal activities; controlled by judgment and reflection, they lead to new discoveries and ever-widening recognition. It is worth reminding ourselves, however, that in a simple and modest way the process of inquiry is the same for the curious amateur as for the scientist. In a less organized way it is the way in which any mind extends its knowledge to become ever more interactive with the world around it. And who has not at some time — if only as a child watching tadpoles in a pond grow legs — enjoyed the rewards of such inquiry, undertaken for no useful purpose, but only to satisfy curiosity? The pleasure is in the pursuit and in the discovery. Think how much of the world's knowledge is in a strict sense "useless," how much of it has been acquired for its own sake, by amateur and scientist alike. It matters to me not at all in any practical way that this heavy, dark rock on my desk — a memento of a morning on a summit in the Rockies — is a piece

of granitic gneiss, sparkling with biotite mica, dotted with orange
lichen, and recording a history of the building up and the wearing
down of a mountain range. Or that this piece of red scoria, idly
picked up from an Oregon lava bed — a stone light in the
hand and full of holes — has a very different history to tell.
But how agreeable to try to read these histories!

Why should it be? The principal reason, doubtless, is that
as human beings we are born to be curious. But another reason,
I suggest, is that learning in this pure sense is detached from
ourselves and therefore gives the pleasure and freedom that go
with absence of self-concern. One key to our enjoyment, I
believe, is that our attention is on something of no consequence
to ourselves. Should we call this activity escape? It might rather
be called freedom and enlargement. If knowledge were only
gained to be put to uses we could foresee, we should by now
have learned very little. Anyhow, for whatever reason, the
accumulation of "useless" knowledge is one of the pleasantest
things in life. It commits us to nothing, it costs us nothing (except
time, and sometimes money, both of which might be worse
spent); it is a pursuit without danger of boredom, and without
any necessary period.

We have not quite finished with our prothonotary warbler
and our other birds. If one of them comes back next spring
we shall have a keener pleasure than just recognition. Its return
will give us the pleasure of recurrence at the same time and
place and therefore a sense of the stability of things. One of the
profoundest pleasures of seconds is just this reassurance — the
reassurance that something will be seen not merely again —
sometime, anytime — but again at a particular time and place,
that it will have a seasonal return to the place in which we first
saw it. Poets have sung about these cyclical returns ever since
there have been poets.

> Somer is i-comen in,
> Loude syng cuckow!
> Groweth seed and bloweth meed

And spryngeth the wode now.
Syng cuckow!

But nearly twenty centuries before this anonymous English poet, the cuckoo had been the sign of spring for the Greek Hesiod. In his *Works and Days* he writes,

> But if thou art late with plowing, remedy hast thou still;
> When, from the leaves of the oak, the cuckoo call is shrill
> For the first time, and gladdens all men to the wide earth's end,
> Then on the third day after, if Zeus vouchsafe to send
> Good rain that fills the hoofprint of an ox — just fills, no more —
> Late ploughers then shall prosper as they that ploughed before.
> But note these things with a mindful heart — mark in their hour
> The signs of the grey spring's coming, and the seasonable shower.

In ancient China, as with us, the movement of wild geese was a sign of seasonal change. For one poet of the T'ang Dynasty (618–906) autumn came when "The first wild goose brushes the Milky Way." These are lines from another poem of the same period:

> A chill wind springs up from the horizon,
> What are your thoughts now, I wonder?
> When will the wild geese arrive?
> Rivers and lakes are big with autumn floods.

These, from still another, called "The Solitary Goose":

> Gaggle upon gaggle return home beyond the frontier pass and are
> gone.
> Why do you wing your way alone?
> Why do you call for your lost comrades?
> Why do you come so late to your winter pool?
> Against the island mist you pass over low in the darkness.

These returns are one of the principal signs of order in our natural world. The recurrent sequence of the seasons, which are changeable in themselves, is itself an order. Spenser's Titaness Mutability, who claims the rule of the terrestrial world, calls as witnesses to her cause the manifestations of time: the seasons, the months, day and night, the hours, life and death, and the planets. When they have passed by in procession, "great dame Nature," called as arbiter of the dispute, denies the claim of Mutability, for although

> all things stedfastnes doe hate
> And changed be: yet being rightly wayd
> They are not changed from their first estate;
> . . . .
> But they raigne over change, and doe their states maintaine.

It is both for acknowledgment of this orderliness and for reassurance to ourselves that we celebrate annual festivals and that we make pilgrimages to our Canterburys and Fujiyamas — even if these be only the hepatica wood in mid-April when the farther lake shore is washed with violet, only the apple barn in October when the maples begin to flame on the hillsides.

At times when agricultural life was more widely experienced than it is now in our industrial Western world and was more central in everyone's consciousness, the year's calendar, known by seasonal signs in the heavens, in weather, and all about in plants and animals, was closely marked by the sequence of work to be done. I have already cited a passage from Hesiod's *Works and Days*, part of which is about the agricultural year. In another such poem, this time from the ancient Chinese *Book of Songs* (800–600 B.C.), the stanzas go round and round the ten months of the Chinese year, sometimes mentioning the weather, sometimes the crops to be planted or harvested, sometimes the pests to be dealt with, sometimes the chores to be seen to. Take this stanza:

> In the seventh month the Fire ebbs [Scorpio sinking];
> In the ninth month I hand out the coats.
> But when the spring days grow warm

And the oriole sings
The girls take their deep baskets
And follow the path under the wall
To gather the soft mulberry-leaves.

Or this:

In the sixth month we eat wild plums and cherries,
In the seventh month we boil mallows and beans.
In the eighth month we dry the dates,
In the tenth month we take the rice
To make with it the spring wine,
So that we may be granted long life.

Our technical skills are continually robbing us of simple, but significant, pleasures in the recurrence of seasonal things like the Chinese poet's wild plums and cherries. What is late spring without that special delicacy which used to come only with it — fresh-picked strawberries? Now that we may have strawberries nearly every month in the year, the edge has been taken off our pleasure in eating them; bred and grown for shipping, they have even lost much of their savor. Marlowe's Doctor Faustus could indeed procure grapes out of season for the Duchess of Anhalt, but to do so was a wonder, and the pleasure was as much in the wonder as in the grapes. It was the rarity, not to say the singularity, of those grapes which enhanced the enjoyment of them. The excitement of having them would soon have dulled had the magic been performed as a daily commonplace. Once we looked forward to chrysanthemums in the fall, their gold and bronze matching the season; now they are the commonest of potted plants the year round in florists' shops. I will have nothing to do with them except when they ought to be there. Irrational? Of course. But the obliteration of seasonal things makes life ever more the same from day to day, makes rare things common, loses for us the expectancy of seldom things.

Allied to this cyclical return of familiar things in season is our return to places we have loved. I have spoken of the hazards of going back to a place of some specially intense experience. But the returns to most places we have enjoyed in a relaxed and everyday way are full of rewards. We know this well enough when we return year after year to some favorite vacation spot. It acquires the comfortable familiarity of old clothes. The second time at a summer place, say at a ranch somewhere in the western mountains, we come back feeling, not strange as at first, but at home, inordinately pleased to find the road in from the highway just as narrow and rough, the ouzel's nest still on the big rock in the creek and the creek roaring with a spring freshet, the dams at the beaver ponds still in good repair, and at the proper turn in the road the peaks gloriously looming at the head of the valley. We shall be disturbed at some changes — such as gas heaters in the cabins instead of wood stoves, the bare place on a slope where a stand of lodgepole pines has been lost to pine rust. We shall be approving of others, such as the strong new bridge, the new corral, the new barn. And as soon as we have dumped our bags we shall be out to see if the horses we best liked to ride are still in the corral, if there are fresh tracks by the salt-lick, if the badger den is down the road, if the pair of snipes is nesting again at the marsh beside the beaver pond.

And on this second visit we learn a good deal more than we did the first time. We are now sophisticated enough to ask more questions. Everybody knows the needle and cone test for the difference between a fir and a spruce, but what is the difference in configuration and color from a distance between fir and spruce, or rather between spruce and spruce and fir and fir? Why is the creek full of granite when the surrounding mountains appear to be all sedimentary limestone and sandstone? Why are there so few spring beauties this summer when last summer there were so many? We bring to bear intervening experience and so we are more observant. Timid guests at the threshold the first time, we become confident possessors the second time of this little world.

You can see, however, why it is important to come back soon.

For we grow possessive of things we remember and if they are gone or altered we feel unsettled, even dislocated. And, indeed, even if they are not materially changed, memory will have made its own romantic adjustments; the visible things when seen again after a long time may appear shrunk and faded. Sometimes the decay is real and we are sorry to have come back. But how could we have known?

My mother and I once found quite by accident a charming guest-ranch near Mecca, in the Imperial Valley of Southern California. It was a date grove and the owners had built three or four adobe guest-rooms. We were for two nights the only guests, and the family gave us dinner in their own big house. We sat by the fire afterwards (for desert nights in February are cold) and the lady of the house told us about the history of their fine experimental ranch, started by her father. She showed us a collection of wild flowers someone in the family had mounted. The guests at the ranch, we were told, were usually naturalists, professional or amateur, who came down in the spring to watch the migrating birds, especially on the national waterfowl refuge at the foot of the Salton Sea. The ranch was a refuge in itself. The date palms, water, a cat's-claw and mesquite thicket, with mistletoe parasitic on the mesquite, brought both resident and wintering birds in abundance — especially Gambel's quail and Gambel's white-crowned sparrows. To the sparrows the mistletoe berries were a gourmet dish. There were also the expected mockingbirds and house finches (as adaptable as English sparrows), Audubon's warblers (common and ubiquitous like their eastern and midwestern cousins, the myrtles), ruby-crowned kinglets, flickers, sparrow hawks, a cactus wren, a buteo (perhaps a Swainson's hawk), a roadrunner (the curious and comic desert cuckoo), and other small birds I could not identify. In the cat's-claw I saw my first black-tailed gnatcatcher, my first verdin, and on the telephone wire I both saw and heard my first phainopepla, a flycatcher of striking black and white pattern.

The vermilion flycatcher that we were told was somewhere about would not show itself. I spent two happy mornings birding before we took off westward to the Borrego Desert and the mountains of our own San Diego County.

Eight years later, when my mother and I had again taken a holiday in the desert, we thought we should like to repeat that agreeable trip. From Mecca we found our way out to the ranch, but grew increasingly apprehensive at the sight of the untended trees, the rusting machinery, the junk, the dogs running about. People of another sort, friendly but slovenly, were in the once neat house. The guest-houses were still there, and clean enough, but now, we learned, kept open only for the duck-hunters in season. We had no choice but to stay overnight, for Mecca, a center for agricultural labor, is hardly a tourist town. We were forlorn at the decay of that beauty and that economy and wished we had not been witnesses to it. The overgrown mistletoe, which had submerged the mesquite, was of a piece with the surroundings. The birds were there, though fewer in numbers and kinds. As special consolation on that disconsolate morning, I saw my first crissal thrasher and heard its beautiful song, less brilliant than the mocker's, softer, muted, more leisurely.

We would not willingly return to a loved place to find the gate off the hinges, the garden overgrown with weeds, the windows broken, the dark corners a habitation of rats. Yet we must take risks. We should be foolish and cowardly to forego for fear of disappointment the rewards of a second visit to a place we had once enjoyed. We have always to reckon with the mutable world. Spenser's Titaness was not wholly wrong: "For, who sees not, that *Time* on all doth prey?" We cannot remain innocents if we would. "O wonder!" exclaims Shakespeare's Miranda,

How many goodly creatures are there here!
How beauteous mankind is! O brave new world
That has such people in't!

To which Prospero replies, "'Tis new to thee." This is not cynicism, but wisdom. Even in the best of our returns, repetition is never wholly repetition, for time's arrow cannot be reversed. We move from experience to experience, weaving the intricate web of discovery and recognition by which we become a part of the world around us and it of us. Yet, though an experience can never be repeated in its particularity, it may be in kind, by ourselves or by someone else. It is this double nature of experience, its particularity and its universality, which makes the world both exciting and knowable. When Miranda and Ferdinand fall in love, to them it is an immense discovery, inconceivable that such a thing has ever happened before or that it ever can again. And, of course, it cannot, to them or to anyone else in precisely the same way. Shakespeare has caught the sense of uniqueness and of the accompanying wonder in the circumstances and dialogue of their first meeting. This I have quoted in part, for another purpose, in the essay on swans. Ferdinand, saved from shipwreck on a strange island and drawn by strange music, thinks he has come upon a goddess. And Miranda, who has never seen a young man, indeed any men but her father and the monstrous Caliban, thinks she is seeing a spirit, "a thing divine." Within moments they know each other mortal and are in love. "This," pleads Miranda to her father, "Is the third man that e'er I saw, the first / That e'er I sigh'd for." The other side, the voice of experience, is spoken by Prospero. "Poor worm! thou art infected," he comments humorously and sympathetically of his daughter. We laugh agreeably with him at this common "disease" of mankind. Hence the double vision in this affair of Ferdinand and Miranda — the wonder of the unique experience, and the awareness that love between young people happens over and over again and makes new beginnings possible to the end of time.

In *Hamlet*, Shakespeare gives us this double quality of experience in a tragic rather than a comic mode. When we first see Hamlet he is in a state of deep grief for his father's recent death. His mother counsels him:

> Do not forever with thy vailed lids
> Seek for thy noble father in the dust.
> Thou know'st 'tis common. All that lives must die,
> Passing through nature to eternity.
>   *Ham.* Ay, madam, it is common.
>   *Queen.*   If it be,
> Why seems it so particular with thee?

Hamlet, stung by his mother's shallowness and insensitivity, picks up the word most important to him: "Seems, madam? Nay, it is. I know not 'seems'." Near the end of the play, in the grave-digger scene, we see Hamlet moralizing on death in its commonness — to politician, lawyer, lady, jester, king — to all men alike. He solves his own dilemma at last by the simple acceptance of the fact of death as a universal experience, for himself as for every man. "If it be now, 'tis not to come; if it be not to come, it will be now; if it be not now, yet it will come: the readiness is all." Without the poet's insight into this double quality of experience there could be neither comedy nor tragedy, indeed no poetry at all.

As creatures with minds we are able to perceive the universal in the particular and unity in multiplicity. Perhaps these perceptions are at the root of our fascination in sitting hour after hour watching the ocean. Every motion of the sea, every heaving wave, every whitecap, every bubble of foam as a wave breaks and rushes toward shore, is unique, itself alone and no other. Yet the sea is always the sea — recognizable, describable, known in its tides every month, every day, every hour, every minute. The creatures of the tide-pools, in the twice-daily rhythm of being overwhelmed by the water and exposed to sun and air, live by this order in change.

We may put our experience of learning, of "firsts" and

"seconds," in another way. We live between the poles of novelty and recurrence, of wonder and habituation to experience, of intuition and reflection, of revelation and doctrine, of romance and everyday. Once in a dozen springs, or in a lifetime, we may be visited by a prothonotary warbler; every spring we welcome our cheerful robins.

Listening

A special pleasure of waking early on spring mornings in Wisconsin, especially if one lives near a wood, is in hearing the increasingly multiple and varying chorus of bird song. One has heard the cardinal off and on from mid-January, and in full morning voice since at least early March. His ringing phrases are the secure ground to which the others will add their own themes and harmonies one by one. At first come the songs, sometimes muted, of the other winter residents — the chickadees, juncos, goldfinches, purple finches, tree sparrows; then the full spring notes of the new arrivals from the earliest in February and March — the mourning doves, robins, and redwings — through all the fine April singers — the white-throats and kinglets, the thrashers and catbirds; then in May the rich-voiced orioles and rose-breasted grosbeaks; and finally on to the last of the May warblers. Each familiar song, heard at its expected time, is as reassuring of the year's renewal as the swelling buds on the trees and as the ground-breaking by the first snowdrops. The absence of one voice is troubling, an uneasy riffling of smooth certainties. Perhaps it is the bright, sweet phrase of the fox sparrow we miss, whose coming has been longed for and whose stay is always short; or perhaps it is the clear "leolay" of the wood thrush, whose move into the wood for the summer has always been taken for granted.

In addition to the reassurance of order in the expected returns there is, I think, a deeper, less conscious renewal of our ties with the natural world. We drift away, in our sophisticated lives, from our ancient diurnal and annual biological rhythms. We insulate ourselves as well as we can against seasonal changes of temperature, and with our late-working, late-rising habits, we put our daily cycle out of phase with the sun and the creatures which live by it. But the swelling chorus of bird song, beginning earlier each day as the spring advances, takes away sleep and even the desire for it; it pulls us back into the cycle of the creatures around us.

> Whan that Aprill with his shoures soote,
> The droghte of March hath perced to the roote,
> . . . .
> And smale foweles maken melodye,
> That slepen al the nyght with open ye
> (So priketh hem nature in hir corages);
> Thanne longen folk to goon on pilgrimages.

And what refreshment of spirit there is in the abundant and manifest energy of those spring songs, whenever heard — the house wren's little flurry of notes flung out every few minutes,

the brown thrasher's rich improvisations, the catbird's less
melodious and even more prolonged kind.

Piquancy is added to these morning listenings with the arrival
of the Baltimore orioles in May. For since every oriole's song
is slightly different in phrasing from every other, one may at
first think he is hearing a new bird altogether until he recognizes
the oriole quality. Moreover, the morning song may change two
or three times as one oriole is succeeded by another until there
is only one which stays to claim the territory. Someone with
a musically trained ear and memory may be able to say if the
claimant is the same bird as last year's. Not I!

Of course, no small part of one's conscious pleasure in listening
to the morning chorus is the pride one takes in being able to
give the right name to every bird in it by its song alone. With
experience gained year after year we come to listen as we would
to an orchestra, when we are alert to recurrent themes, changes
of key, interesting intervals, the special qualities of different
instruments — in short, when we deepen our musical pleasure
with more discriminating attention.

Recognition of the singers may seem to be a less important
satisfaction than those others I have been speaking of. But to
consider it for a moment will serve to make a point about listening, not only to birds, but to other things. For me there is
a heightened pleasure in learning to identify birds by the ear
alone, without the aid of sight, perhaps just because it is harder
for me to do. Perhaps it is harder for many others as well. For
one thing, given no major defect which cannot be overcome,
such as color blindness, the keenness of sight is largely a matter
of degree and therefore can be sharpened by glasses and
binoculars, whereas with hearing, however acute, there are more
qualitative variables to take account of. For another thing, with
seeing, the recognition pattern is perceived instantaneously, in
space; whereas with hearing the pattern is perceived sequen-
tially, in time. For whatever reasons, the recollection of a song

heard may for most people be less reliable than the recollection of a bird seen. Certainly the aids to recognition we find in the field guides are in the nature of things far less satisfactory for hearing than for sight. Long ago W. H. Hudson wrote a shrewd essay on the futility of trying to represent bird songs by any means of translation or notation. Translation of the notes of a song into spelled-out syllables or into words or phrases is of course strictly impossible, and when attempts at it do sometimes prove helpful, as with "Peabody, Peabody" for the song of the white-throated sparrow, they are so through suggestion rather than equivalence. The described qualities of a song, often useful as supplementary evidence to more reliable signs, do not take us very far in actual identification. "It is easy to say," Hudson wrote, "that a song is long or short, varied or monotonous, that a note is sweet, clear, mellow, strong, weak, loud, shrill, sharp, and so on; but from all this we get no idea of the distinctive character of the sound, since these words describe only class, or generic qualities, not the specific and individual." He was himself, as readers of his accounts of English and South American birds will remember with delight, extraordinarily sensitive in describing the qualities of bird songs.

Even recordings have their limitations as aids to recognition. Anyone who has listened to a recording of a succession of sparrows, say, or warblers, in one of Peterson's *Field Guides* and has tried to find that particular sparrow or warbler he heard on his morning walk, will know that recordings may be as frustrating as books. The reason, of course, is different from the inadequacy of notation, for this difficulty lies in the human ear and memory. The chief difficulty is probably that the context of the original hearing has been lost. The buzzy little warbler song we were puzzled by was heard off and on among other warbler songs, many greatly varying in quality and pattern, some only slightly. We thought we had, nevertheless, the troublesome

one firmly fixed in mind. But when the separate songs pass by
us in review and we attend to them one by one we lose the
memory of our sought-for phrase. Nothing seems quite right.
We know that to listen discriminatingly to a bird's song —
to hear its distinctive phrases and tones, to separate it from
others, to fix it in memory — requires great attentiveness. In
this attentive listening I think there is a more profound satisfaction than in just recognizing or learning the song, and it has
to do with the listening itself. To be silent, to be attentive to
something outside oneself, especially to empty one's mind of
self-concern and of irrelevancies, as one has to do in listening
(more, perhaps, than in looking), is a fine capability of the human
mind, and one that can be cultivated to our pleasure and profit.
The listening may be not only to sounds. We may, for instance,
listen with even greater attentiveness to silence. In his famous
account of the idle time he spent in the Patagonian desert, when
his mind was empty of thought, Hudson speaks of listening to
the silence, and he describes his state as one of suspense and
watchfulness.

It is hard for us in these latter days to find silences to listen
to, for the roar of mechanical noise pursues us on the ground
or in the air nearly anywhere we go, no less in the deserts than
in the cities. But we must all of us at one time or another have
listened to silence and have experienced the concentrated attentiveness which goes with such listening — the listening for something in the stillness, the willing out of it the slightest murmur
of insect, or rustle of leaf, or sigh of air. Such sounds as come
are startling and distinct. The silence itself becomes a presence,
as if it had a sound of its own beyond the utmost reach of our
hearing. I remember as a small child sitting alone in an attic
bedroom. No morning sounds at all came from the house below.
A door from the bedroom was open to the storage part of the
attic, always a mysterious, silent place where nothing ever
moved or happened. In the great stillness, I heard my heart

beating. Perhaps I only felt it, but the effect was of hearing it, as if it were outside myself — regular, loud, and solemn. I was not frightened, only awed by the silence and the single sound it summoned out of itself. For the mind's ear to listen with such intentness and at the same time with detachment from self may be, I suppose, a first step towards mystical contemplation. Of that I do not wish to speak in ignorance. Nor am I really thinking of so extreme and special an exercise. I am thinking of a wider, more general sort of combined attentiveness and detachment — call it "detached attentiveness," or "attentive detachment," as you will. The mind's ability to listen to other voices than its own, to reflect on something other than the needs of its own body, is what makes man free. Man's memory and foresight, his capacity both to learn and to plan, do not necessarily take him beyond his economic and political world. His power to be still and to listen may.

Scientific observation is one way to exercise this ability to listen, sociological another, linguistic another, and so on through various fields of observation. But the ability may also be exercised in listening to the past as well as to the present. Man is the only animal, presumably, which can contemplate its own history and be instructed by it. And he can be, not just through learning directly what to do or what not to do, but, more significantly, through enlarging his comprehension of himself as man.

The burden of much that Loren Eiseley writes in his essays on man's evolutionary past is that man makes his future out of what he understands, or misunderstands, of his past — not only his historical past, but also his past in becoming man, something modern scientific inquiry has made partly known to him. In a fine passage in *The Unexpected Universe*, Eiseley uses the listening metaphor. He likens modern man in his universe to an orb spider at the center of its web, "fingering the universe

against the sky." The web which man has spun with his knowledge extends "through the starry reaches of sidereal space, as
well as backward into the dark realm of pre-history." With his
telescope and his radio he extends his seeing and hearing into
immense distances; with his electron miscroscope, into the most
minute structures of himself. "It is a web no creature of earth
has ever spun before. Like the orb spider, man lies at the heart
of it, listening. Knowledge has given him the memory of earth's
history beyond the time of his emergence," and he reaches forward with his new machines into a future beyond his own life.
It is essential that he listen well and truly to his evolutionary
past lest he determine a future for mankind which will be self-
defeating.

Such remote reaches of the past are not for me to speak of.
I must speak of the nearer past and the more limited things
in it I know about. Those are the voices of poets and story-tellers,
uncountable times nearer to us than the first men and part of
our immediate literary heritage, yet requiring of us a listening
effort if we are to hear truly what they had to say. For not
only do social and intellectual climates change with time; but
language, even if it is our own, also changes. It is less the obvious
changes than the subtle ones to which we must be most attentive.
In some ways a poet very far off in time is less likely to be
misunderstood than one nearer to us — Homer, for instance,
than Shakespeare.

Homer, in a different language (which we must therefore learn
or have translated for us), speaks of a world so remote from
our twentieth-century western European or American one that
we readily take him on his own terms. Shakespeare, apparently
in our language (and therefore one we think we need not learn),
speaks of a world nearly enough like ours to tempt us to read
him as if it were altogether the same. But how much we miss
when we do! We may, if we wish to, have a Marxist *Romeo
and Juliet*, a Kottian *Midsummer Night's Dream*, a fascist (or

anti-fascist) *Julius Caesar*, a Freudian *Hamlet*, an existentialist *Lear*. We can seize the plays as therapy or as propaganda for our times. But if we use them in these ways, their essence will escape us, though we may be too ignorant or insensitive to realize that it is doing so.

It is a curious thing. We would not be reading Shakespeare, or putting him on the stage, if his plays did not move us and come home to us, not just in an insight here and there, but in their vitality as artistic wholes, in which story, character, setting, thought, and poetry are all cooperating parts. Why, then, are we so casually disrespectful of their creator's intent? Shakespeare's characters are so sensitively and imaginatively conceived that they attract us as if they were living people. Yet, quite perversely, we often fail to listen closely to the very speeches which make them seem so. It is a pity to cram all of Shakespeare's vital and indescribable Hamlet — with his intense passions, his inconsistencies, his savagery and generosity, his mistrusts and his loyalties, his doubts and his probing questions, his ranging mind, his brilliant wit, his fierce honesty — into a narrow psychiatric case study, an anachronistic one at that. Besides, how do you psychoanalyze a figment of an artist's imagination? It is deeply imperceptive to level the terrible grandeur of *King Lear*, with its cataclysmic upheavals in the macrocosm and the microcosm, its intense suffering and its ineffable tenderness, to an existential flatness; to turn its fiery positives into gray negatives; above all to blur the margin between its unmistakable evil and its unmistakable good.

Is it that we cannot understand Shakespeare's language and his art? or that we do not wish to? It is true that much in the moral world assumed in his plays has gone from our world or is in the way of going — respect for authority based on age, position, and knowledge; distinctions of respect and privilege marked in courtesies and ceremonies; naturalness and sacredness in social bonds, as in marriage; obligations and loyalties in relations between "master" and "servant"; absolutes in the conception of good and evil. It is true that Shakespeare's noblest characters express sentiments of patriotic or personal honor which to young modern ears sound flamboyant or unconvincing; true that his young lovers suffer torments of longing and voice poetic fancies which our young people find quaint or just plain silly; true that the simplicity with which chastity, honesty, and truth are conceived seems to many strange or even incomprehensible. But we cannot read these things out of him and not be the poorer. If we have not listened, what have we let him tell us, as only he could, about human experience? How have we from his rich store of wisdom enlarged our own understanding of what men have suffered for, and lived by, and died for? what dreams they have had, what moments of insight or blindness? what cruelties they have inflicted, what kindnesses they have shared? what follies or what nonsense they have laughed at? what moral dilemmas have led them to tragedy? what reconciliations, to comedy? For these are the things poets, Shakespeare among them, not so much tell us, as make us feel and know; but their instruments must be their own language and their own art. If these have retreated from us in time, we must make an imaginative leap to reach them, or as much of them as we can, lest we miss forever that wisdom and that beauty. There is a kind of stultifying arrogance in thinking that all truth is ours and only newly discovered by us.

A man, by virtue of being human, has the ability to listen with sympathetic interest, and without self-interest, to another voice than his own, to someone speaking of other circumstances than his, perhaps in different words than he would himself speak. Respect for another mind and sympathy with it may open the door to understanding and to the sharing of a vicarious experience of a different sort from his own. By a leap of sympathetic imagination he can cross barriers of upbringing and education, of economic and social status, of age and sex, of nationality and race, of time, and even — with help — of language. He cannot do these things easily, or always completely, but even to wish to make the attempt is a capability of the human mind not to be lightly regarded, for by this effort the mind can travel abroad or backwards in time, and be forever the richer and wiser.

In speaking only of Shakespeare's, or any poet's, meanings, I have been guilty of some distortion, for we hear the meaning through the poetry and by means of it, not apart from it. Our listening is not merely metaphorical, for how a thing is said is as important as what is said, and poets have music to be heard with the ears as well as the mind. Let me illustrate the point from *Romeo and Juliet*, which is so lyric a play in mood; in it the love sings. But the singing is highly artful — "artificial," the Elizabethans would have said, meaning no dispraise, for what we say must be clothed in appropriate form both to please and to persuade. The lovers always speak in formal, often bejeweled, verse, rich with metaphors and imaginative conceits. Here is Romeo in the Capulet garden looking up at Juliet in her window:

> Two of the fairest stars in all the heaven,
> Having some business, do entreat her eyes
> To twinkle in their spheres till they return.
> What if her eyes were there, they in her head?
> The brightness of her cheek would shame those stars
> As daylight doth a lamp; her eyes in heaven
> Would through the airy region stream so bright
> That birds would sing and think it were not night.

And this is Juliet, waiting impatiently for her wedding night:

> Gallop apace, you fiery-footed steeds,
> Towards Phoebus' lodging! Such a wagoner
> As Phaëton would whip you to the West
> And bring in cloudy night immediately.
> . . . .
>   Come, civil night,
> Thou sober-suited matron, all in black,

And learn me how to lose a winning match,
Play'd for a pair of stainless maidenhoods.
Hood my unmann'd blood, bating in my cheeks,
With thy black mantle till strange love, grown bold,
Think true love acted simple modesty.

This is hardly the "natural" language of lovers, and is not meant
to be. It is rather the distilled essence of the emotion, which
is lyric in impulse; it gives form to the "idea" of young love
in its intensity and beauty, and at the same time to the sense
of uniqueness in the experience of just these two.

What the love poetry does, in the play as Shakespeare wrote
it, we may appreciate better if we think of the Zeffirelli motion-
picture version of *Romeo and Juliet*, in which a great deal is
cut out of the speeches in favor of much passionate love-making
between a teen-age boy and girl. Long speeches are an embar-
rassment to film-makers because they hold up action. Moreover,
language is not needed to create the moods that go with setting
and time of day — "Lady, by yonder blessed moon I
swear, / That tips with silver all these fruit-tree tops" — for the
camera provides the orchard and the moonlight. The eye may
be so filled with the splendors of Italian Renaissance public
squares, churches, and palace interiors that the ear does not
hear properly what is said even when Shakespeare's lines are
left in. Seeing is substituted for listening, not least in the love-
making. Kisses are many, words are few. The Zeffirelli film gives
us an intense drama of adolescent love, but the adolescents might
be any other two; the drama is charming, winning, greatly
moving, yet in important ways not Shakespeare's *Romeo and
Juliet*. What we get is the story, almost reduced to its essentials
— the unhappy fate of a boy and girl whose love was "star-
crossed" by senseless family enmity; just as a story it is fool-proof
and perennial. It was old and successful before Shakespeare
dramatized it and is as appealing now as ever. But Shakespeare
intensified and enriched the simple story in many ways — in

management of plot and setting, changes of timing, greatly
developed characters, a new rôle for Mercutio, and, not least,
full exploitation of his poetic medium. His stage play, written
so largely for the ear, probably cannot be transferred without
loss to the emphatically visual medium of the film. Another handsome film version, Castellani's, also tended, by various cuts and
changes of emphasis, to suppress some of the peculiarly Shakespearian features of the play and to make it more like the basic
Italian tale widely known in the sixteenth century.

I shall speak only of the effect of Shakespeare's love poetry,
which is largely replaced in the Zeffirelli film by the love-making
itself. The difference in the handling may be said to be one
of style. But the difference is more than in manner alone, for
the style is the vehicle of attitude and meaning: the difference
in styles is therefore profound in its effect. In Shakespeare's
poetry is expressed or implied not alone physical desire, but
also worship, beauty, idealism, the whole discovery of first love.
You will recall that when Romeo first meets Juliet at the Capulet
ball and falls in love with her, their first dialogue is in the form
of a charming sonnet, the parts of which are shared between
them, and the couplet is wittily closed with a kiss.

> *Rom.* If I profane with my unworthiest hand
> This holy shrine, the gentle fine is this:
> My lips, two blushing pilgrims, ready stand
> To smooth that rough touch with a tender kiss.
> *Jul.* Good pilgrim, you do wrong your hand too much,
> Which mannerly devotion shows in this;
> For saints have hands that pilgrims' hands do touch,
> And palm to palm is holy palmers' kiss.
> *Rom.* Have not saints lips, and holy palmers too?
> *Jul.* Ay, pilgrim, lips that they must use in pray'r.
> *Rom.* O then, dear saint, let lips do what hands do!
> They pray; grant thou, lest faith turn to despair.
> *Jul.* Saints do not move, though grant for prayers' sake.
> *Rom.* Then move not while my prayer's effect I take. [*Kisses her*]

Thus from my lips, by thine my sin is purg'd.
Jul. Then have my lips the sin that they have took.
Rom. Sin from my lips? O trespass sweetly urg'd!
Give me my sin again.
Jul.   You kiss by th' book.   [*Kisses her*]

The running image, of a pilgrim worshipping at the shrine of
a saint, catches the young man's feeling of adoration. But it also
allows the wooing game to begin. Romeo takes the lead, and
Juliet is a quick follower, though properly shy as well. In the
interchange, the controlled and witty game holds in the excitement of their mutual discovery; it makes for boldness, yet keeps
it within the bounds of propriety.

In the next meeting, when Romeo "with love's light wings
. . . o'er perch[es]" the walls of the Capulet orchard and sees
Juliet at her window, there is no embrace; all the developing
passion is in the poetry.

Jul. By whose direction found'st thou out this place?
Rom. By love, that first did prompt me to enquire.
He lent me counsel, and I lent him eyes.
I am no pilot; yet, wert thou as far
As that vast shore wash'd with the farthest sea,
I would adventure for such merchandise.

The dark overtones of the tragedy to come are there too. It
is Juliet who has the premonitions.

Although I joy in thee,
I have no joy of this contract to-night.
It is too rash, too unadvis'd, too sudden;
Too like the lightning, which doth cease to be
Ere one can say 'It lightens.' Sweet, good night!
This bud of love, by summer's ripening breath,
May prove a beauteous flow'r when next we meet.
Good night, good night!

Outright sensuality is left to verbal expression by other characters — to the coarse-minded Nurse, to whom one man is as good as another, and to the witty, worldly Mercutio, who mocks Romeo's former sentimental love-sickness for Rosalind, but who never knows about his genuine passion for Juliet. By this means the love of Romeo and Juliet is set apart in its speciality and completeness. The meeting of the lovers at Friar Laurence's cell for the marriage is brief and formal. When we next see them together it is at their parting in the early morning after the wedding night. For his killing of Tybalt, Romeo has been banished and must leave Verona by daybreak. These last moments of his with Juliet are therefore intensely poignant. But like the dialogue of meeting, the dialogue of leave-taking is restrained by the form. We see the lovers, not on a bed or in a bedroom, but from the garden, at Juliet's window, as Romeo saw Juliet on the night of wooing. They speak in a balancing pattern of contradiction, antithesis, and final paradox, using the traditional theme of the aubade or dawn-song, the lover's reluctant parting from his lady at daybreak. The lark and the nightingale, moreover, were the most familiar poetic symbols of morning and evening. Here, as in the wooing sonnet, Shakespeare's form and imagery enrich the moment with overtones of a long literary past.

> *Jul.* Wilt thou be gone? It is not yet near day.
> It was the nightingale, and not the lark,
> That pierc'd the fearful hollow of thine ear.
> Nightly she sings on yond pomegranate tree.
> Believe me, love, it was the nightingale.
> *Rom.* It was the lark, the herald of the morn;
> No nightingale. Look, love, what envious streaks
> Do lace the severing clouds in yonder East.
> Night's candles are burnt out, and jocund day
> Stands tiptoe on the misty mountain tops.
> I must be gone and live, or stay and die.

At Juliet's pleading, Romeo joins her in denying the daylight

and the lark. "Come, death, and welcome! . . . Let's talk; it is not day." But his reversal, and the full realization of what
it means, brings about hers: it is not day. Hie hence, be gone, away!

and the lark. "Come, death, and welcome! . . . Let's talk; it
is not day." But his reversal, and the full realization of what
it means, brings about hers:

> It is, it is! Hie hence, be gone, away!
> It is the lark that sings so out of tune,
> Straining harsh discords and unpleasing sharps.
> . . . .
> . . . arm from arm that voice doth us affray,
> Hunting thee hence with hunt's-up to the day!
> O, now be gone! More light and light it grows.
>   *Rom.* More light and light — more dark and dark our woes!

Here the passion contained is far greater than in the meeting
sonnet; the danger is not just a cloud on the future, but
imminent; the full irony of the lovers' situation is experienced.
The coming tragedy casts its shadow before it. When Romeo
has climbed down from the window, Juliet sees his face below
"as one dead in the bottom of a tomb." Shakespeare in no way
lessens the physical side of the love by not fully displaying it;
he only respects the intimacy of both the desire and the grief.
The poignancy is all the greater for the restraint. In the formality
of the parting, the painful, raw experience is given dignity and
beauty; it is elevated above the immediate personal emotion
of these two dramatic characters to the level of universal
experience.

Shakespeare wrote *Romeo and Juliet* fairly early in his career.
His later love poetry is less decorated and less formal. The
rhythms are subtler, but they are still lyric. The poetry functions
in the same way to contain and elevate the passion. And in it
there is felt an even greater pressure to reach the perfect "idea"
of the love and of the beloved. Here in *The Winter's Tale* is
Florizel's praise of Perdita, the supposed shepherdess:

>   What you do
> Still betters what is done. When you speak, sweet,
> I'ld have you do it ever. When you sing,
> I'ld have you buy and sell so; so give alms;

Pray so; and for the ord'ring your affairs,
To sing them too. When you do dance, I wish you
A wave o' th' sea, that you might ever do
Nothing but that; move still, still so,
And own no other function. Each your doing,
So singular in each particular,
Crowns what you are doing in the present deed,
That all your acts are queens.

And here, Cleopatra's lament for the dead Antony:

O see, my women,
The crown o' th' earth doth melt. My lord!
O, wither'd is the garland of the war,
The soldier's pole is fall'n! Young boys and girls
Are level now with men. The odds is gone,
And there is nothing left remarkable
Beneath the visiting moon.

Shakespeare's language of absolutes, expressing the reach towards excellence, towards the ideal in goodness or beauty or love, is thoroughly Elizabethan and growing strange to modern ears: "Admir'd Miranda! / Indeed the top of admiration, worth / What's dearest to the world!" The "ideal" of our time is the mediocre — the average man, not the best man; the ordinary experience, not the extraordinary. Listen to Marlowe in *Tamburlaine*:

What is beauty, saith my sufferings, then?
If all the pens that ever poets held
Had fed the feeling of their masters' thoughts,
And every sweetness that inspir'd their hearts,
Their minds and muses on admired themes;
If all the heavenly quintessence they still
From their immortal flowers of poesy,
Wherein as in a mirror we perceive
The highest reaches of a human wit —
If these had made one poem's period,

And all combin'd in beauty's worthiness,

Yet should there hover in their restless heads
One thought, one grace, one wonder, at the least,
Which into words no virtue can digest.

The climbing note, the ascending scale, the reach for the top, always just beyond reach, is the music of Shakespeare's time, not of ours. We seem to prefer middle C.

At the close of the essay in which Eiseley uses the metaphor of man as a spider at the center of his web, he returns to the metaphor of listening. Man, "the self-fabricator," he says, surely did not come across an ice age to see in "the mirrors and magic of science . . . himself or his wild visage only. He came because he is at heart a listener and a searcher for some transcendent realm beyond himself."

In Shakespeare the moments of transcendence come at profound moments in human relationships, and they are like grace. When Pericles, after years of searching, has found his lost daughter, he hears strange music:

> *Per.*
> . . . I am wild in my beholding.
> O heavens bless my girl! [*Music*] But hark, what music?
> Tell Helicanus, my Marina, tell him
> O'er, point by point, for yet he seems to doubt,
> How sure you are my daughter. But what music?
> *Hel.* My lord, I hear none.
> *Per.* None?
> The music of the spheres! List, my Marina.

We have come a long way from the morning chorus of bird song. Or have we?

A Solemnity

The episode recalled at the end of this essay took place in the early fifties. If at that time one were to stand on a certain hill to the east of Desert Hot Springs in the Colorado Desert and were to pick just the right spot, a rise of ground to the west would quite shut out the view of the small town. (The hill, with an oasis of native palms below it, was called Miracle Hill for its two springs, one of hot and one of cold water.) And if one had one's back to the Little San Bernardinos, the low tawny range to the northeast, one would look southwest across a great stretch of empty desert to the mass of San Jacinto Mountain. One knew that Palm Springs, unseen

at this distance, lay at its foot; that a main highway from Los
Angeles carried through the pass between San Jacinto and San
Gorgonio a heavy stream of traffic to the Colorado River and
beyond, and, on the hither side of the river, to the heavily cultivated parts of the desert, the date groves and the market gar-
dens reaching south to the Mexican border. One knew, too,
that smaller roads and the grids of little settlements were all
about. Yet from this vantage point, the small risings and fallings
away of the ground in the seeming plain concealed nearly all
man-made features and produced the illusion of great emptiness.
Glimpses of the railroad, marked by the water-tower at a junc-
tion, the pylons swinging a power line off to the west from
Parker Dam, tamarisk windbreaks marking occasional dwellings
only emphasized the seldomness of man's presence in the
immensity. These things were still so a few years later, when
I again stood above this little oasis, facing the great bulk of San
Jacinto. Probably now even the illusion of emptiness is gone,
so busily and speedily have men possessed the Southern California desert. Like creeping knot-grass putting down roots as it
spreads, they have quite overlaid it. When I was first there,
they had settled on its western parts only as the little desert
sand-mats do, fitfully, here and there, easily pulled up by the
single root. But men's transformation of the land they sought
as an escape from metropolitanism is another story.

Back to our mountain, there still in the old way no matter
what lies at its foot. Men living in the neighborhood of a promi-
nent peak are always magnetized by it. They look towards it
when they rise in the morning; during the day they glance up
at it from time to time without thinking much about it; and
at evening, in the last light, they try to hold it with their eyes
from the effacing blackness. Waking on a moonless night, they
will even strain to make out its shape, vaguely uneasy that its
presence is no longer manifest. Now San Jacinto stands at the
western edge of the Colorado Desert like a great presence. The

inhabitants of Palm Springs, being right at his feet, have him at their backs, and if they turn they never get a look at anything but the gullies and ragged scrub of his lower slopes; whereas the dwellers in Desert Hot Springs always have the whole eastern side of him in their sights.

If I could choose a mountain for every day, I believe I should choose San Jacinto. Like his patron in the calendar of saints, he has no great fame in the catalogue of mountains. His elevation of slightly better than ten and three-quarter thousand feet excludes him from the company of the Mount Whitneys and Rainiers, the Long's and Pike's Peaks, let alone the McKinleys. He even stands about six hundred feet lower than his rival, San Gorgonio, across the pass to the north in the San Bernardino Range. Yet in effect he does not, because there is no softening foreground of foothills to break the rise, as before San Gorgonio. San Jacinto comes right out of the desert floor, all ten and a half thousand feet of him above ground, for the desert at Palm Springs has only about four hundred feet of elevation. This sudden lift to such a height gives the mountain an impressiveness beyond what one would expect from the elevation figures on the map. The bases of our greater peaks in the Rockies are high above sea level before they begin their upward thrust, and those in the ranges nearer the coast are often obscured by foothills so that their full height is seen only from a distance. Not that San Jacinto is spectacular in the way the Grand Tetons are, lifting their sheer rock faces above Jackson Hole. They leap up, those El Greco mountains, sharp-angled, tall, and reaching. Not so San Jacinto. He sits, massive, his great knees and feet spread apart, his crown rounded, his shoulders wide. The big buttresses which hold up the mass extend out into the desert like the forelegs and paws of the Sphinx (if one may allow the Sphinx three forelegs instead of two), and, like the Sphinx's paws, they rest on it clean — at least that is the illusion from ten miles or so, too far for the plantings of the fringing towns to be noticed.

Hence, from Desert Hot Springs, the whole of San Jacinto's bigness is in sight, and it is to him one's eyes turn without volition rather than to the gentler and half-hidden San Gorgonio. San Jacinto suggests protective strength, not awfulness or aspiration. His might is for his desert valley.

Who was San Jacinto, or Saint Hyacinth, that a mountain in California should be named after him? And who, San Gorgonio, commemorated in the companion peak? Since there were two Saints Gorgonius and eight Saints Hyacinthus — none of either among the greater saints — the answer is not as simple as it might seem. And the identification, if we could make it, would not perhaps matter much anyhow. Yet the question invites us to take a backward look to the time, remote in spirit if not in years, when the captains and missionaries of New Spain sprinkled this California country with holy names as they pushed northwest from Mexico. Perhaps I shall be forgiven for a speculative digression — one not, I think, wholly impertinent — before returning to the mountain itself, the desert, and my small adventure therein.

It was customary for the explorers to call any marked feature of the landscape, such as a spring, a hill, or a bay, after the saint on or near whose day they came upon it and camped near it. Thus, San Diego has its name because Vizcaino sailed into the bay on November 10, 1602; he called it after the Spanish Franciscan saint, San Diego de Alcalá, whose feast day was November twelfth, the day on which a thanksgiving mass was said. In this way Vizcaino had been charting and naming the harbors and islands up the coast of Baja California, and in this way he continued up to the highest latitude he reached, somewhere between forty-one and forty-three degrees, along the northern California or southern Oregon coast, leaving unrolled behind him a geographical calendar of holy days. The Roman liturgical calendar of feast days, modified for Spanish dioceses, would have been the readiest as well as the most proper source of names. There were exceptions, of course, as when a descriptive name was given, such as "Baia de Ballenas" for one of the "ensenadas" or open bays in Baja California where the gray whales congregate for calving and breeding. The naming, one supposes, would normally be the responsibility of the chaplain of the expedition.

Father Crespi, with the Portolá land expedition up the coast from San Diego to San Francisco in 1769 and an associate of Father Serra for many years in the founding of the chain of missions, is said to have bestowed more names on the map of California than any other single person.

One might expect, therefore, to find the names of San Gorgonio and San Jacinto Mountains in one of the many journals kept by the captains and their priests as in the third quarter of the eighteenth century they opened land routes from Sonora across deserts and mountains to the coast of Alta California. But apparently none of the diarists of these journeys has recorded any naming of these peaks — not Father Palou, with Governor Fagés in 1772 on a hunt in the back country for runaway Indians from the San Diego Mission; not Father Díaz, Father Palou, Father Garcés, or Captain Juan Bautista de Anza himself on his great trail-making journey through the San Jacinto country in the spring of 1774 or again on the same route (this time with Father Palou, Father Eixarch, and Father Font) in the fall and winter of 1775; and not Father Garcés on his own in 1775–76, when he crossed the San Bernardino Mountains from the north and headed down the valley to San Gabriel. The expeditionists named valleys and streams freely enough as they went along, but though they spoke of the sierras, or ranges, along which they traveled or over which they crossed, they did not distinguish individual peaks. Mountain peaks are of course much harder to be sure of than bays, since their shapes alter and their topographical relations appear to change with the point of view of the observer.

Our peaks must pretty certainly, then (unless omission from

a diary was by inadvertence), have had their christening later. | 59
The names are first heard of as the names of mission cattle
ranches — Rancho San Jacinto in 1821, of the San Luis Rey
Mission; Rancho San Gorgonio in 1824, of the San Gabriel Mission. It would have been unusual, however, if the peaks had
been named, as has been supposed, after the ranchos rather
than the other way about.

Without help from the records, therefore, we have to sift the
names in the calendar as best we can. Both of the Saints Gorgonius belong to that frequent class of obscure early martyrs
who have no identity beyond their martyrdom and who may
share even that in pairs or triplets — the Saints Cosmas-and-
Damian of the martyrology, remembered as one. The Saint Gorgonius whose day is March eleventh is joined with Saint Firmus,
and nothing precise is known about the two. The Saint Gorgonius
whose day is September ninth is paired with Saint Dorotheus.
Chamberlains of Diocletian at his court in Nicomedia, they were
martyred about 300, and their existence is attested to by
Eusebius and Saint Jerome. We read, among their acts, how,
roasting on a gridiron, "they lay thereupon as they had lain upon
a bed full of flowers and suffered none harm."

As for the Hyacinths, they, too, sometimes come with insepa-
rable companions, and there is only one among the eight whose
existence and some of whose acts are credibly verified; that is
Saint Hyacinth (or Jaczko) of Poland, whose day was August sixteenth (now seventeenth). He was a thirteenth-century Dominican (vested in his habit by Saint Dominic himself), stout of body
and spirit, who carried the faith into distant and alien places,
to Scandinavia, to Kiev, even, it was said, to the borders of
Tibet and to Grand Tartary. The other Hyacinths are little more
than names, their days scattered throughout the year, except
for the one whose acts, shared with his companion Saint Protus,
are embedded in the story of the learned and spirited Roman
virgin, Saint Eugenia. We may read in Caxton's English version

of the *Legenda Aurea* of Jacobus de Voragine (that wonderful collection of saints' lives which was favorite reading in the Middle Ages and a treasure house for preachers) of Eugenia's astounding education in the liberal arts and in philosophy, of her sudden conversion in Alexandria, at fifteen, to Christianity, her rejection of pagan learning and persuasion of her companions in study, "Prothus and Jacinctus," to do likewise, and of their all joining a community of monks, she in disguise as a man. Little more is said of Prothus and Jacinctus until their beheading in Rome for refusal to worship idols is told at the end of the story. Eugenia's trials and martyrdom, after three survivals of attempted drowning, burning, and starvation at the command of the Roman Emperor, surpass in detail and interest those of her old companions.

The interesting thing is that *this* Saint Hyacinth's day falls on September eleventh. In the *Golden Legend*, the story of Saints Protus and Hyacinth follows immediately after the story of Saints Gorgonius and Dorotheus, whose day is September ninth. When I found them thus in sequence together, I was certain I had found the patrons of our pair of mountains, seen on some September journey, perhaps up from San Diego or out from San Gabriel. The Anza expeditions were of course ruled out by their dates, March–May of 1774, December of 1775.

Compilers of the place-name dictionaries allow this Gorgonius, all right, but not this Hyacinth. Their choice for the patron of San Jacinto Mountain is the historical Saint Hyacinth of Cracow. He would indeed have been a fitting saint to be chosen by the namers of this mountain outpost in a heathen land. But associative reasons of this sort were not the kind operative in the Spaniards' naming process. And historical authenticity, beyond the testimony of the calendar itself, would not have been thought of. With some exceptions, as when a saint was singled out for special honor (like the naming of the great bay to the north and its presidio for the Franciscans' own patron, Saint Francis of Assisi), names were bestowed according to the chance of the calendar. A saint on his day was called on to receive a new honor, and with it a new obligation. Great or small, he could thenceforth touch that spot of land and its people with blessings. The place and the nature of his own blessedness were of no importance. So Saint Patrick was summoned from green Ireland to cast an eye on a rough and desolate canyon, "San Patricio," in which the Anza party camped on their way up from the desert on March 17, 1774. And we must assume, without other evidence, that whichever of the Hyacinths — whether the Dominican of Cracow, the martyr of Alexandria, or some other — the patron of our San Jacinto Mountain may be, he is so by the accident of his holy day. From this point of view his identity is not even significant.

Such a conclusion is in itself interesting, however, for it marks an extreme difference in the Spanish way and our way of bestowing names on new geographical discoveries — ours egocentric, theirs caelocentric. Ours are given for personal glory or for sentiment. The ranges of Antarctica have the names not just of the discoverers but of the discoverers' wives and friends; and so are many of the newly found features of the moon likely to have. The Spaniards sometimes bestowed names for personal glory, too, though rather for the glory of a patron than of themselves — as, for example, Monterey, to honor the Conde de Monte Rey, viceroy of New Spain when the bay was discovered in 1602. But for the most part they peopled the California terrain and shore with a heavenly host, as stable and abiding in memory, it would have seemed, as terra firma itself. And to the greatest and the least of the angels and saints they boldly gave a share in the responsibility for the new land. How many times more ceremonial and more melodious, too, were their names than ours — "el Pueblo de Reina de los Angeles sobre el río de Portiúncula," "la Sierra Madre de Santa Cruz," "la Misión de San Luis Rey de Francia," "la Misión del Santo Arcángel San Gabriel de los Temblores," "la Misión de Nuestro Seráfico Padre San Francisco de Asís a la Laguna de los Dolores" — our vulgate "Frisco"! The Spaniards' San Gorgonio has become our commonplace Grayback, their San Antonio our trite Mt. Baldy. Back for a moment to Saint Hyacinth of Rome and Alexandria, and then we shall have done with the saint and return to the mountain. If he is indeed our San Jacinto, we have started a very small hare. All the same, one is teased by the exotic names of Gorgonio and Jacinto, names to us without meaning or association. And one tries, by pausing on them a moment, to open a reach of history, whether in the adventures of the strangers who first brought European languages and customs into this alien land, or whether in the minds of these and earlier Europeans who nourished their faith on tales of heroism and wonder in the hagiographies.

Our Gorgons and Hyacinths and their companions are in the class of saints who, for want of reliable records, have been shorn of their claims to sanctity by the Vatican, or at least demoted by losing their holy days. The witness of Eusebius and Jerome may have saved Gorgonius of Nicomedia, but one doubts if Hyacinth of Rome and Alexandria will have survived erasure. The reasons for dropping such names from the calendar of the liturgical year are obvious enough. Celebrations of their feasts can hardly serve a religious purpose if they have become little more than names. And if they are famous in name, but dubious in their acts, their trials of spirit and their martyrdoms are too remote from the temper of modern times, the simplicity and wonder of their stories too alien to modern idiom, to serve an exemplary purpose. Still, one is troubled somewhat by the insistence on applying "fact" as a test to this world of wonders, by the narrowness with which credibility is interpreted.

The life of Saint Eugenia and her companions is a case in point. Some time ago the Reverend Sabine Baring-Gould, in his *Lives of the Saints*, noted that the story of the three "belongs to the domain of legend, not to history," and that it is "full of ridiculous anachronisms and impossibilities." After observing that there was no bishop named Philip (Eugenia's converted father) in Alexandria in the third century, he commented, "Papebroeck, the Bollandist, says that instead of these Acts proving to be gold, they are mere dross, and Tillemont says they are fable and fiction." Fable, yes. But dross? For whom? Not for the listeners for whom the tale was told, listeners more accustomed to moving in a mental world in which a less certain line was drawn between fact and fiction and one in which truth could appear in many symbolic guises. Even interpretation of the Bible was not confined to the literalness which came to be the first principle of Reformation and post-Reformation criticism. The saints' lives could be understood, enjoyed, and profited from without being believed in to the last detail; belief in them was never required as an article of faith. To deny their validity because they do not meet modern standards of credibility is to mistake the premiss on which they were based, which is that faith works wonders. To test such stories by historical evidence would seem to be as mistaken as to try to prove the existence, or non-existence, of the Loch Ness monster by photography or by dragging the lake. And why, even for us, should the saints' legends be dross? If they can no longer serve an exemplary purpose, they still bear gold within them, though it may be akin to the gold of fairy-tale. We can do without the unremarkable Saints Gorgonius and Hyacinth, even, perhaps, the quite remarkable Saint Eugenia. But it wouild be a pity to lose from the inherited riches of our imaginations Saint Jerome's faithful lion, Saint Anthony's tempting centaur, Saint Brendan's marvelous voyaging, and perhaps Saint George and Saint Christopher altogether. If we cannot respond to their legends with pleasure and sympathy, we shall soon be unable to read *The Faerie Queene*, even *Cymbeline* or *The Tempest*, not to mention the Bible. We shall have to begin to purge the text, first, of Joshua's trumpets, Gideon's pitchers, Elijah's raven, Jesus' loaves and fishes, then of more consequential things, and where shall we end? From time to time men go through these sober cleansings of the irrational from the things they believe and affirm. But the irrational and the wondrous, in old or new forms, always turn up again. Perhaps the passion for scientific accuracy is only skin-deep. Witchcraft and astrology, never quite dead, are being resuscitated by a science-indoctrinated college generation. And some among us are inventing substitutes for the older wonders — much poorer ones, others of us would say. The little green men from outer space are remarkable chiefly for their greater engineering powers than ours — and we seem to be catching up even with those.

The Spanish captains and missionaries who overlaid the California countryside with holy and melodious names were troubled with no such doubts about the saints. Their names, ceremonious in themselves and bestowed with ceremony, gave grace and sanctity to an unwelcoming land. For in its natural state, little-watered and semi-desert, Southern California was no garden spot. The Indians who lived upon it, and by it — the Indians whose souls the friars came to save and who were not always willing to have them saved — lived sparely, without agriculture. On the coastal side of the mountains, the western Diegueños, Luiseños, and Gabrieliños lived on the berries and seeds of the chaparral (the "little forest" of shrubs covering the hills), on the fruit of the cactus, on acorns from the live oaks and mesa oaks, on grasshoppers, grubs, and such small game as quail, lizards, rabbits, wood-rats and ground-squirrels. On the desert side, for the eastern Diegueños and Cahuillas, the fare was less abundant, though adequate, the same in kind though different in particulars — mesquite and cat's-claw beans, for instance, in place of acorns, more lizards and chuckawallas and fewer rodents. The Luiseños and Cahuillas who lived about San Jacinto perhaps knew the mountain as "Takwish," for the spirit who lived there, an evil

spirit who manifested himself in meteors and in ball lightning.
Still, its canyons and slopes offered a place of escape from desert
heat, of larger and more abundant game (deer and mountain
sheep), of fresh springs and streams of water. It had another
kind of spring as well. On the desert side, in a long cleft, there
was an oasis of palms and a hot spring of healing water; two
other mineral springs, one hot and one cold, flowed at the foot
of the western slope. Indeed, a whole series of hot springs, precious to the Indians, bubbled up along the lines of faults, all
the way down into Baja California.

This is a long digression, all begun on account of San Jacinto,
that bold mountain with the exotic name. On that day in the
desert, I was to look up and see some flying objects, too —
better, I think, than flying saucers. I must return to my small
adventure.

I was saying that at that time, nearly a score of years ago,
one was still conscious, in spite of increasing settlement, of great
emptiness in this corner of the Colorado Desert. One could,
by wandering away from roads, lose one's life without effort,
if not without distress; indeed one may do so still. Few years
pass, even now, without someone, lost and waterless, dying in
some part of the desert, even in proximity to well-traveled roads.
From Desert Hot Springs it was then possible to find solitude
easily and quickly. One had only to drive up to the Aqueduct
Road, which in this neighborhood ran close to the foot of the
Little San Bernardinos along the line of the Los Angeles aqueduct
coming across the range from the Parker Dam to the east on
the Colorado. Or one could drive along the narrow ribbon of
Dillon Road curving along the foot of the same range southeast
to Indio. In either case one met little traffic. From these roads,
with the car parked, one could explore afoot a bay in the hills,
like the one where grew the pure stand of Bigelow chollas, a
photographic temptation of form and color, brown and silver
and chartreuse; or one could work up one of the gullies which

may be entered from a wide dry arroyo or wash at the foot and which often lead up into narrower ravines. These are watercourses cut by the run-off in desert flash-floods, seldom but powerful. Over the centuries the gullies have deepened and have collected a detritus of rocks washed from the sides or from above. Here at the untidy foot of the mountains, in the "unswept stone besmeared with sluttish time," are rock-hounds' treasure troves. And the dry arroyos, because of dampness at greater or less depth beneath the surface of the sand, are fine places for living things, too.

On this morning of April twenty-third I chose to explore such a wash, a rather narrow one with the sides soon closing into form a little canyon. None of the small things I noticed was out of the ordinary, except to me, who was the merest novice at observation in the desert. Earlier in the month, the canyon bed would have been rich in flowers, but now only a few plants were still in bloom: little gold-poppies, their yellow flowers no bigger than rue anemones; a bush of white ratany, its tiny purplish-red pea flowers nested in the angular gray twigs and giving off their delicious raspberry scent; an indigo bush, another of the pea family, with flowers darkly blue; desert gilia, close to the ground, its lavender flowers delicately streaked and softly borne in woolly cups; heart-leaved evening primroses, tall-stocked, with closed yellow blooms, interesting less in themselves than in bearing witness to the abundant varying of their genus in the desert; blue and lavender phacelia, too, of several kinds — another family that here proliferates its species. Antelope squirrels fussed shrilly at me from their burrows in the canyon walls. Looking up, I noticed in a long niche a packrat's nest of oddments well stuck together with round green cholla joints. The usual desert birds were about — house finches twittering and busy, a mourning dove gleaning swiftly on the sand, a pair of desert sparrows calling to each other sharply in warning, a buteo sailing over, a hidden rock wren singing its

loud "chew, chew, chew," canyon wrens ringing out their
descending scales. I was still uncertain about these two wrens,
so swift-moving and elusive are they; I counted it good luck
to be sure for the first time of actually having seen a canyon
wren. I had not the same luck with the thrasher. While I was
sitting on a boulder at the mouth of the wash, I heard a bird
I could just see, not clearly enough to make sure of. The song
was full and varied, a lovely song, new, but certainly a thrasher's,
and frustrating. In this idle way, I poked about, absorbed, working up the little canyon. For a while, each time I looked back,
San Jacinto was framed by the walls in a new perspective. Then
on a turn I lost it. The walls, closer and higher, shut out the
peak.

I had no sense of passing time until the cord which ties us
by habit to hour and place — to the noon hour, to waiting family,
this time to a car on the road — began to tighten. And here,
in this place, there was something else, the uneasiness of the
tenderfoot; its backward pull began to grow as strong as the forward pull of curiosity. Anyhow, it was getting very hot in that cleft
away from the breeze, and I had found enough treasures for the
morning.

I glanced up between the canyon sides at the sky, perhaps
to guess the hour, and saw a wonder — strange motes far up
in the shimmering brightness; white wings, black-tipped, circling
in a solemn dance, scarcely to be distinguished from the sky
in that blazing light. If it had not been for the black, momentarily
lost and seen again, I might never have noticed anything. What
could these creatures be? Not snow geese, which never had
such a spread of wing or would use it so. Unhurried, with slow
wingbeats and a long glide, each following the other, those
twenty or so great birds kept their formal circle — like Botticelli's
angels circling above the ruined stable and about the throne
of God. The binoculars told me what they were. Though I could
not, in that light, make out precise details of form, I could see the

proportions of small tail and large head. And I caught glimpses of pink. The birds could only be white pelicans. The pink through which the light glowed on some turn was the pouch-skin under the bill.

They were pelicans on their spring migration, no doubt, from their wintering place to the south on the lower Colorado River, or some coastal lagoon on the Gulf of California, to some northern lake, perhaps Pyramid Lake in Nevada, where on Anaho Island they would lay their eggs and brood their young. The pelicans of Anaho are used to long flights, for in the nesting season many of them journey sixty miles twice a day — from Pyramid Lake to the Stillwater Refuge to fish, then back again with the catch for their nestlings. But on this morning's flight there was no need for haste. Before the urgency of family duties should begin, this was a ceremonial progress. The strong fountain of warm air springing up from the mountains sustained them and they danced in hymeneal solemnity. These were not random revels. For as certainly as the orbiting moon is carried forward on the earth's path around the sun, the pelicans in their circling moved north, unhurriedly, but steadily. How many times had the Cahuillas, the old inhabitants of these mountains, or other Indians before them, looked up at the pelicans on their habitual spring journey? And how long before the Indians appeared in this empty land had the pelicans circled above it? They are ancient birds.

I turned and clambered back down the little canyon. When I made the sharp turn, San Jacinto and his great knees came back into view.

The
Desert Sparrow

Do not wait eagerly for the desert sparrow, for he will not appear until the end, and then in no dramatic way. He is in any case a small bird, with a small song, soberly feathered and somewhat elusive. This essay has more to do with the habits of people than of birds. But place is most important in it, and the place is Desert Hot Springs, the scene of the pelicans' migratory flight described in the preceding essay.

Some years ago, during a leave from the University, I took an April holiday in this little town. I did not seek it to "take the waters" or bathe in the hot springs for which it is named, as most outsiders go to it to do, but only to spend an idle and restorative week or two in the desert. I had been in the place with my family in February and had picked it as most suited to my needs. The town was very small, yet because of the springs offered plenty of accommodations for strangers. The sandy, flowering desert floor was within a few minutes walk of any point in it. A road along the foot of the hills and another higher up along the line of the Los Angeles aqueduct made other kinds of topography quickly accessible by car. During my holiday fortnight, however, the weather turned uncooperative, as it has a way of doing in the desert spring. Stiff, cold winds blowing sand made outdoor rambling impossible for about half the time, and being forced to stay indoors I learned more about the town and the people, in gossip with the woman who rented me a cottage, than I should otherwise have done. Although Desert Hot Springs has grown greatly in area and population since that spring, the reflections its earlier state suggested will not now be impertinent. Quite the contrary, I think. For what struck me about it so forcibly was the way in which its residents were even then innocently, but busily, undermining the very things they valued — or said they valued — the desert for. The more who come to build the faster the undermining. Let me first sketch the setting — the desert, the town, the people.

If one comes to the Colorado Desert by car from Los Angeles, the direction from which most people come to it, one enters it through a natural gateway between the peak of San Gorgonio on the left hand to the north and the peak of San Jacinto on the right hand to the south. One enters the desert, then, at its northwest corner. If he curves to the right around the base of San Jacinto, he will shortly come to Palm Springs, of great fame. If he turns to the left around the base of San Gorgonio, he will be on a road headed for a pass between the San Bernardinos and the Little San Bernardinos, the mountains dividing the Colorado Desert from the Mojave Desert to the north. But if instead of going through the pass, he stays on the hither side of the range and turns straight east he will come to Desert Hot Springs, of little fame. Indeed, it is known (or used to be known) as "the poor man's Palm Springs." Its situation is meaner than its neighboring resort town, but its view is grander, for the gateway peaks to the west and southwest are far enough away to be seen; whereas the residents of Palm Springs, closely backed by their own great mountain, face the flat desert.

I remember that one morning at sunrise I looked outside to see a piece of rainbow in the west. Just the partial glimpse above the frustrating houses in my street was so startling that I got into the car and drove to the east of town, where a road wound up to a small height and a view point. From there the little town at my feet seemed only a bright wave-edge on the immense empty stretch to the mountains in the west. In the retreating slate-blue cloud mass, a complete rainbow, its piers on the plain, arched across the snowy top of Gorgonio, touched by sunlight. For more regular and substantial fare, I could look every day to the mass and height of San Jacinto.

The more level parts of the Colorado Desert are what is known as creosote bush desert. That is, the dominant shrub is the creosote bush, sometimes called greasewood, but most truly and affectionately, by the Mexicans, *hediondillo* or "little stinker." The size and spacing of the bushes is a sign of the degree of aridity of the desert floor; they are healthy and large (as high as five or six feet), but well spaced out, around Desert Hot Springs. Their dark green foliage relieves the desert of any general grayness, even in the non-flowering seasons. In the spring, they are covered with yellow bloom, and later in the season with small white fuzzy balls. Scattered among the creosote bushes grow several kinds of smaller bushes, such as burro-bush, a composite with inconspicuous yellow flowers, and brittle-bush or *incienso*, a greenish-gray floury-leaved shrub with a showy rounded crown of yellow daisy-like blossoms. Most interesting to the novice observer in the desert — at least to this novice — are the numbers and kinds of small flowering plants, which make of the desert floor in a good year a *mille-fleurs* tapestry. The blooms come in many kinds and colors — evening primroses, forget-me-nots, and pincushions of several sorts, desert lilies, desert chicory — all in white or cream; desert gold-poppies, desert dandelions, desert sunflowers, other composites, and other evening primroses in yellows and golds; lupines, gilias, and phacelias in blues, violet-blues, lavenders, pinks, and purples. Some plants, so small and inconspicuous in themselves as not to be noticed except by a searching eye, have special charms — perhaps in the fascination which intricacy of design executed on so minute a scale has for us, perhaps in the piquant incongruity we perceive in the survival of such fragility and daintiness in so harsh a world. Among these miniatures are the white-rayed, yellow-centered Mohave desert-stars, the rosy-red purple mats and silvery-white frost-mats, the asymmetric, ruby-spotted blossoms of desert calico. Because these tiny flowers can only be properly examined on one's hands and knees, they are inelegantly, and somewhat contemptuously, known by the local people as "belly-flowers." This lovely diversity, less striking in color at a distance than the dunes near Palm Springs, which are overspread with rose-purple sand-verbenas and creamy dune-primroses, was the special spring characteristic of the flat stretches around Desert Hot Springs. In the early evenings, small flocks of pale Brewer's sparrows, enthusiastically trilling their buzzy, variable song, swarmed from one creosote bush to the next. And at any time of day Gambel's white-crowned sparrows, hastily feeding and on the move, might sing over and over their one quick, bright phrase.

In the midst of this living abundance the little town was squared off in a grid of eight or ten streets each way laid out by the compass. The town center was formed by the crossing of the east-west road in and out of town with the north-south main street leading up to the principal bathhouse. At the crossing and along the main street might be found the businesses of the town — a couple of gas stations, a two-story hotel, a drug store, two grocery stores (one a small model of a supermarket and selling liquor), a counter café, a coffee-shop with tables, a movie-house, a post-office. I do not recall a bank, but I suppose there must have been one; if there was not then, there would soon be. The community appeared to be as well supplied with spiritual as with creature comforts, for it had three churches — a Methodist, a Baptist, and a Catholic. I shall have something to say about these in a moment.

The dwellings up and down the streets were of two sorts — modest little residential houses of frame or stucco, and cottage courts or motels, also modest but pleasantly laid out, for the more abundant visitors. The several mineral hot springs were the ultimate source of the town's prosperity. The steaming pool in the biggest bathhouse was daily filled with soaking bodies, too close-packed to swim, even if the enervating heat left them enough energy to be able to. There were rooms besides for private baths and massage. Two other bathhouses, a little farther out, did not lack for customers either. The working residents of the town who had no direct business interest in the springs made their living by them indirectly, by renting rooms and cottages or by providing necessary goods and services. There were, of course, non-working residents, too, usually elderly and arthritic, who like nearly everybody else had come for the sun and the dry air and the comforting waters.

A few fancier motels, with swimming-pools, were springing up, and bigger and costlier residences were being built farther out and higher up on the rise of the foothills. Desert Hot Springs was acquiring its suburbs. To the northwest, for instance, on higher ground, a speculator had graded and paved roads, put in lights and sewer, and was grandly advertising the district as "Cholla Estates." The expensive houses were being built in

stands of the bristling Bigelow cholla cactus, handsome to look
at, deadly to get close to. (It was in the Cholla Estates that
I had my first excruciating lesson in the ways of the "jumping"
cholla.) In contrast, the town itself had not caught up to these
Palm Springs airs. It still seemed simple enough. To the northeast, against the hills, lived an eccentric of sorts — artist, adven-
turer, "discoverer" of the place, or nearly so. It was he, after
many years with the Eskimos in Aslaska, who had settled near
the beneficent springs and had built himself an idiosyncratic
house of stone, piped only with hot water from his own well.
He showed the house and his Alaskan treasures to visitors,
preached the healing virtues of the water, and painted desert
landscapes. "Miracle Hill" was his name for the height above
the little oasis of palms where flowed two springs, one hot and
one cold.

There must have been other, more private, eccentrics in the
town or in the hills, for such a place draws them. The odd thing
was that there seemed to be so few. The signs were all of the
commonplace. What struck me forcibly was the safe and unad-
venturous ordinariness of a community of people set down in
an extraordinary natural setting in which nothing — not climate,
or scenery, or the lives of the wild creatures — was either moder-
ate or safe. I ought not to have been surprised, for these people,
mostly middle-aged and older, had come to such a place for
health and comfort, not for adventure. Furthermore, they were
like most settlers in transplanting their own kind of society to
the new environment. Still, those I talked with, like other desert
dwellers in other communities lacking Desert Hot Springs'
peculiar asset, professed that the desert attracted them greatly
as a place in which to live, and they seemed unaware that to
live in it in their way would inevitably transform its most
desirable, even some of its essential, features into something
quite different. Simple as the place seemed, therefore, quite
without Palm Springs' luxury, a powerful and unrecognized process of irreversible sophistication was at work.

The appeal of the desert as a place to make one's home in is in the dryness and clarity of its air, the magnificence of its night sky filled with elsewhere forgotten stars, the tenacious and prodigal beauty of its wild things, its immense spaces and silences and the sense of remoteness from the world's hurly-burly which these give. The inhabitants of Desert Hot Springs put these things more simply. They said they had come because they liked the desert and saw it as a way of escape from the rush, the traffic, the noise, and the smog of Los Angeles or of the cities within its orbit. Yet to make life in the desert comfortable, or even tolerable, the settlers had brought Los Angeles with them — not, of course, its cultural amenities but its mechanical ones, its internal combustion engines, its washers and air-conditioners, its lawns and trees and cultivated herbage. Besides its conveniences they had also brought its Kiwanis and Rotary Clubs, its kind of chamber of commerce. In short, they had planted its seeds for reproducing itself. What more need be said? The humidity was going up, the daytime heat was growing oppressive, the stars were dimming. Before long the people in the town would hear no more the night sounds of coyote, fox, and owl. Just as new desert communities had sprouted to the south of Palm Springs, each pretending to beauty, exclusiveness, and privacy while at the same time being tied to a roaring highway lined with neon lights, motels, drive-ins, and juke boxes, so Desert Hot Springs would send out shoots of hillside "developments" bending southeast with the Dillon Road and reaching for the old resorts and date groves far to the south. In a few years the whole of the Colorado Desert would be laced with highways and much of the time would lie under a brown haze. A night traveler would scarcely ever be out of sight of twinkling lights.

The yearning to escape from the city to nature, whether the nature be wilderness or merely "the country," is recurrent in the experience of civilized Western man. But he must always face the same dilemma. If it is wilderness he wants, he cannot invade it and still preserve it. Probably he does not often really choose true wilderness, that is, choose it without intending to accommodate it in some measure to himself. Certainly the people of Desert Hot Springs had not so chosen. Doubtless it was natural enough for them to make their town as much like the towns they had come from as they could. They could hardly have been happy except within their familiar social pattern.

This pattern was nowhere more evident than in the town's religious life, which was dominantly Protestant, therefore potentially schismatic. I said I should say something about the three churches. It will not be much; yet I think there is a kernel of interest in the little I was able to observe about them. The Methodist church was the biggest, the nearest the center of town, and from the looks of the congregation the most fashionable — so far as fashion went in Desert Hot Springs. The Catholic church, several blocks from the crossroads, was smaller, less well attended and certainly less fashionable. The rather gloomy priest, making do on scarcely enough income to pay his housekeeper and feed himself, had evidently been rusticated to this small desert parish to cure a chronically infected ear. I cannot recall what the Baptist church building was like, but I learned that the life of the members was at that moment active and intense, for the congregation had just been split by a schism. So here one could recognize a small model, even though incomplete, of the social pattern of Southern Californian and even midwestern religious life.

Of the split in the Baptist congregation I learned from my landlady, one of the schismatics, or at least one who had chosen, perhaps only for sociability, to cast in her lot with that party. She was not dogmatic or heated on the subject, but she told me that feelings ran high among many of the others. The quarrel had been about a new preacher, whom one group in the congregation had disapproved of. What was objectionable about him escapes my memory at this distance of time, but it had to do

with his theological views, which were either too liberal or not
liberal enough. Anyhow, the dissenters withdrew, thereby losing
the right to use the church building and having to meet for
services in the house of one of their members. But loss was
matched with gain, for if they had lost the building they had
carried away with them its electric bells, equipped with several
hymn tunes as well as chimes. The splinter group were planning
great things, no less than a bigger church right up town, in
which the bells would be installed; and they had even then a
new preacher on trial. I do not know the end of the story,
whether the schism was healed, or whether the cutting from
the parent plant took root and grew strong; and if so whether
the parent survived the shock.

The next Sunday was Easter, and my landlady urged me to
attend the public Easter sunrise service which the new congregation was going to conduct on an open rise of ground to the north
of town. The precious electric bells, the card up its sleeve, would
call to worship all the people in Desert Hot Springs and round
about.

At the first faint light of dawn on Easter morning I heard
the bells, though faintly. I arose and dressed, in two minds
whether to attend the service or not. But as soon as I was in
the car, I knew where I was going, for the quiet air and the
early hour were too precious to lose. I skirted the site of the
meeting and headed uphill to one of the inspection stations on
the aqueduct. It was at the mouth of a wide wash which I had
explored before. I knew that here in the sand there were sometimes special rewards for the searcher — tall phacelias with deep
blue-violet bells, sand blazing stars with shining petals of pale
cream, perhaps even a fragile ghost-flower, scarcely to be seen
against the sand except for the fine crimson streaks on its ragged
white petals. And as early in the morning as this there should
be birds. Farther up in the wash I had one day seen a number
of different kinds, including warblers unfamiliar to me. While

78 | I was attentive to the ground at my feet, alert for flowers, I heard the light sweet trill of a desert sparrow. I recognized it readily enough, for I had several times heard it at a distance, but the singers had always proved elusive, moving farther up the hillside from one bush to another. This time I resolved to stay quiet and be patient. After a while the singer came closer and performed on a twig not a dozen feet from me. There in the growing light he perched, neat in his dark gray and white suit, and swelling his black throat with song; he finished each one with soft little turns and variations. These, not heard at a distance, go undescribed in the bird books. The rising sun, hidden from me by a shoulder of the hill I was on, filled the valley with light. From below, the sound of the worshipers' first hymn came faintly up to me. My little sparrow moved off up the hillside, carrying his own small song farther away. I accepted the morning's gift as sufficient for the day and went down from the hill.

A
Postcard from Delphi

It was a postcard from Delphi in the spring of 1968 which began this rumination. The postcard had on it a view of the ancient ruined Temple of Apollo set in the rocky fold of Parnassus, and my correspondent wrote that on the day of his visit eagles were soaring above the cliffs and thunder was rumbling in the gorges below. He could not help being moved, as if the place had never lost its holy mysteries.

That same spring, I, too, paid a holiday visit to a place of harsh and splendid mountain scenery — to the "ghost" mining town of Oatman in the Black Mountains of northwestern Arizona, a range running parallel to the Colorado River for about ninety miles south from the Hoover Dam. I had come to Oatman, as I had come several times before, for a certain kind of refreshment. It is a good place for my kind of idling — rambling about looking for rocks and birds and flowers, or gathering bits of geological and mineral and historical lore from my miner uncle. I find it pleasant to sit on the terrace towards evening watching the sunset glow deepen the reds and purples in the surrounding mountains and, for a few moments of startling clarity, bring every contour and hollow close. I probably should not have thought of Oatman in any special way except for the postcard from Delphi.

The Black Mountain country is beautiful in a stark way. It is a volcanic landscape, formed for the most part of several Tertiary lava flows of different mineral composition, and much altered by erosion between these events and afterwards. Oatman lies along the winding Gold Road after it has dropped from the pass over the range into lesser hills. The buildings of the town, strung along the road and scattered about the hillsides, are set against an immense backdrop of reddish-brown rock, weathered into irregular ridges, peaks, and buttes. One of the things exposed by erosion is an intrusive rock of different color, a great pointed crag, pale and buff-colored, thrust up against the skyline. This, the Elephant's Tooth, is the dominant feature of the place. The curving and descending road leads out of the town, through lessening buttes, past the cusp of the Boundary Cone, and down the long detrital slope westward to "the River."

The vegetation on valley and hillside is desert vegetation — sparse, scrubby, prickly, and gray-green in exposed places, brighter green and denser along the watercourses. Life is lived by both plants and animals under what seem to us to be harsh conditions. But the house finch, building her nest within the spines of a jumping cholla (which has the most cruelly efficient spines of any cactus), is as unconscious of the harshness as a robin in the midwest is of the precariousness of her nest on

the ledge of a second-story window. Living things in the desert,
though spaced out, are few neither in kind nor in number. There
is as much variety of kinds of living things and as many individuals as the environment will sustain and as are sufficient to ensure
the continuance of the species. This means, in fact, an abundance
in the desert, even in a more formidable desert than Oatman,
always surprising to a greenland dweller. My essay, however,
is not about the wild life of Oatman, except as it is part of the
landscape.

The fierce wild beauty of the natural landscape has a special
interest in this place because man has tampered with it in a
special way. In the years before and after the First World War,
men came in the thousands to dig for gold, and though the miners
have gone except for a handful, the country outside the town
is strewn with their leavings: half-ruined, eyeless cabins, with
dark sockets for windows; a fenced graveyard with rough board
markers at the two-score or so of weedy mounds; yellow tailings
at the mouths of mines; sudden deep pits with treacherous, cav-
ing sides; old head-frames, derricks, trolleys; and lying all about
a detritus of rusting iron, broken glass, and old rubber, resistant
to decay and absorption. Away from the town there is a great
stillness. A guy-wire creaking in the wind, a loose roof of cor-
rugated iron suddenly reverberating, are startling and spooky.
The wild things, both animal and vegetable, are at home again.
In the spring, all sorts of yellow composites, desert dandelions,
orange poppies, apricot mallows, purple phacelias, magenta and
chartreuse cactus blossoms ornament the tires and the gasoline
drums with incongruous vitality. Among rocks and shrubs, birds
sing and nest — cactus wrens and rock wrens, Scott's orioles,
ash-throated flycatchers, Say's phoebes, gilded flickers, hum-
mingbirds, mourning doves, house finches, desert sparrows.
Gambel's quail crow in alarm and race with their queues of chicks
into the heaps of ruins.

Not least at home in these littered places are the small native burros, once the prospectors' indispensable pack-animals, which have returned to their natural wildness and multiplied. They thrive on the scant browse. All day and all night in the spring the raucous braying of the jackasses echoes among the tailings and the buttes. You may see a little herd of eight or ten on a hillside moving deftly in single file along a narrow trail, or otherwise going about their spring business — the jennies grazing while a loudly complaining jack is driven off by the new lord of the herd. Or you may hear them at night quietly walking past the window to drink at the little sump made by a dripping pipe behind the house. They are more often, however, the observers than the observed. You may happen to look up and see along a ridge above your head a line of gray, white-ringed muzzles, sharp eyes and sharp ears, all focused (for who knows how long?) on yourself. They are beautiful creatures in their wild state — well fleshed out, with sleek coats, ranging in color from light gray to black, but all with light bellies and the wide white ring around the gray nose, and nearly all marked on the back with a dark cross. They step along briskly and are wary and independent, not at all like the poor depressed creatures, small, thin, and half-asleep, which one sees in Mexican border towns, where they stand at a corner all day suffering their pictures to be taken with American tourists on their backs.

> Who hath sent out the wild ass free?
> Or who hath loosed the bands of the wild ass?
> Whose house I have made the wilderness,
> And the barren land his dwellings.
> He scorneth the multitude of the city,
> Neither regardeth he the crying of the driver.
> The range of the mountains is his pasture,
> And he searcheth out every green thing.

This, then, is the look of things around Oatman.

The town has a past — therefore a "history" — very close to the present. The people in the town live in abandoned miners'

houses or in new ones often partly built of salvage from the
old. This kind of assimilation is, we know, a process often
repeated in history — one Troy, one Jericho, one Verulamium
or Bath overlaps the preceding one, built from it and upon it.
Many a medieval European villein used Roman bricks to build
his cottage or his byre. In Oatman one has a chance — in a
modest way, to be sure — to see the tearing down and the
building up. There is, of course, a radical difference between
an economically vital city and a ghost town which is not quite
a ghost — a town which people keep alive for the sake of health
or remoteness from commerce or old habit or who knows what
idiosyncrasy. Apart from this, the important difference of Oatman from these old cities is that all the history of the Arizona
town has occurred just now; there is no perspective distance
to it, no continuous past stretching back through a long history
to a time before history.

The importance of this fact can be understood if one thinks
of the landscape of a country such as Ireland. There, every few
miles, as one drives along, one glimpses through hedge-openings
or across moorlands the ruin of a round tower, a castle, or a
church. The commonest ruins belong to a well-defined time and
cause, the Cromwellian campaigns and occupation of the mid-
seventeenth century; from the European point of view these
are recent ruins. But from much older times, from the early
centuries of Irish Christianity (the fifth to, say, the tenth), there
are also abundant relics — the stone beehive houses of the first
monastic communities (as at Clonmacnoise or on the Skelligs
off the Kerry coast), the ruins of hermit cells on the western
islands, the high crosses standing in still-used graveyards or mar-
ketplaces. And beyond these yet again are the remains of pagan
times, themselves stretching from the foundations of the great
banqueting hall on the hill of Tara (the Irish Mycenae, the center
of the principal heroic legends) back to the standing stones and
burial mounds of early bronze-age people in the Boyne valley,

and farther still to stone-age graves as old as 6000 B.C. Although anthropologists have little to go on in interpreting these most ancient prehistoric cultures, one is not conscious of a total break between them and historical times. The interesting thing is that there is continuity in decorative design between the art of the ancient inhabitants and the art of the Celtic peoples who came, apparently, in the first century A.D.; perhaps less unexpectedly there is continuity also between pagan and Christian Celtic designs. Consequently, Irish Christian art touches hands with a very ancient past. At the near end of the long vista of the past, the physical evidences of very recent history — the Easter Rising of 1916 and "the Troubles" of 1919–22 — are also sometimes visible, at least in monuments, and are anyhow strong in memory, ready to be recalled by every Irishman. There has been a continuing tradition of saga and legend, even to the present; ancient beliefs and half-beliefs are still alive in folklore and in poetry. Such a tradition is cumulative. The long past is caught up into the present; old and recent things, the reminders of which are visible side by side, seem almost contemporaneous. The driver on a tour bus will describe to you with equal immediacy of detail the fighting at the Post Office in Upper O'Connell Street in 1916 and the Battle of the Boyne in 1690. His interest may flag a little when you arrive at the tenth-century high crosses of Monasterboice or at the four-thousand-year-old tumulus at New Grange in County Meath. There is nothing "ghostly," however, about any of the past, and the long-continued turbulent history has not ended, is not just now even quiescent.

After Ireland (or Britain or Greece or Asia Minor) the history of a small western American desert town seems slight indeed. I am not forgetting that in the lower Colorado basin there are prehistoric remains, too. Human occupation did not begin with the American miners of the late decades of the last century. There were Indians there, the Mohaves and the Yumas (whose people still live about the country in greatly diminished numbers), and before them there had been others, perhaps more than one people, leaving behind them signs of occupation in arrowheads and shaped stone tools; metates (mortars) and manos (pestles), where on the surface of a boulder or stone floor of a cave they had ground mesquite beans; graves containing beads, broken pots, and bits of chewed yucca fiber; petroglyphs and pictographs on rock faces. By some unknown people, immense human effigies were scraped out on the surface of the mesas to the east of the Colorado in southwestern Arizona, and were only within recent years discovered by modern white men from the air. Without a view from above, indeed, their form cannot readily be apprehended. But all these signs of Indian occupation have to be looked for; unlike the ruins of Irish buildings they are non-declarative, non-visible to the casual traveler. These Indians lived lightly on the land, in tune with it, changing it little. And between the Indians, even those still living, and the American white men, there is complete discontinuity. The study of the Indian remains is an antiquarian interest for archaeologists, anthropologists, and amateur dabblers in these subjects, things far away and long ago and having nothing to do with us. What the prehistoric Indians of this region have left behind is little indeed, and very hard to interpret. Moreover, the living Indians know as little of these earlier cultures as we do. They cannot read the geometrical designs carved on the rocks, know nothing of the great figures spread out on the mesas.

Hence, in a place like Oatman, a sense of antiquity is almost absent. It is not true that a sense of history is absent, because a small group of people living there are intensely interested in the events and personalities of the mining days. What they have to go on is only partly reliable. Anecdotes, sometimes true, sometimes not, and improving in the telling, abound. Outsiders, especially, have sentimental notions about old miners, and there is always an old-timer willing to embroider a tale to suit his listeners. Surviving objects, such as a miner's candlestick or pan, are given exaggerated importance and sought for as collectors' items. In the center of town a post with a lateral braced arm at the top, from which as a kind of emblem a miner's bucket hangs, can readily become in the imagination a gallows where bandits were strung up. But Oatman has no history of banditry; nothing in its past resembles Tombstone, where the Earps flourished. When the history is factually accurate, gathered from mine records, old newspapers, and the like, it is all centered about the mines, lost mines or the takings of actual mines, hence about the marketplace and about personalities. It is immediate, everyday stuff and can be lively and interesting. But naturally enough there are no causes in it, no religion, and little if any poetry. The immediate past is all there is, regarded with either a historian's or a story-teller's eye. The western American imaginative genius is for the prose anecdote and the tall tale, as important to the cultural history of a place as factual event, and it takes time for these to gather around a node to form a legend. Given the modern pace and the modern temper, it may be too late for legends anyhow — as much too late as for mythology. In any case, a poetic idiom is not available in our day for the legendary and the heroic.

But human beings seem to need a past and one that has in it something that can be romanticized and glorified. Perhaps this need for something more remote and more romantic is what lies behind the importation of London Bridge, recently rebuilt over a diverted channel of the Colorado at Lake Havasu. The immediate aim of the bridge is money-making; Lake Havasu City is a multimillion-dollar promotion scheme, an "instant city," and the resort on the lake is the last word in commercially slick holiday-making, everything about it unrelated to the stern land-scape. The bringing of the bridge to this place is incongruous in the last degree. It would be comic if it were not so shockingly impertinent. History, or romance, cannot be brought with the stones, even if they were the right stones. As if this ancient living river and more ancient rocks needed more than their own dramatic history! By one who has the knowledge the steps of the history can be read with special clarity and fullness, because in this place until very recently men had done little to alter or to overlay the natural features of the country and hence to obscure the geological story.

Yet the question teases. Would this particular form of advertising even have been thought of if there were not felt some vague sense of inadequacy? the thing that makes Americans abroad so taken with the mere age of things, to the amusement of Europeans? It may be that in places of such formidable scenery (and only scenery), where the contours are angular, and where green, the fruitful color, is largely absent — it may be that in such places we miss something, perhaps the sense of a lived-in land. When we are not awed or exhilarated by such an impersonal landscape, we may find the emptiness in time as well as in space disturbing.

Or perhaps what is lacking is the numinous. The white man feels no mysterious other-worldly presence at Lake Havasu or Oatman. Special features of landscape like river gorges, caverns, or mountain peaks have always been terrible and holy — Delphi, the grotto at Lake Cumae, Croagh Patrick, Mount Sinai. Oatman is set in a country like Seir or the Sinai Peninsula. In the part-circle of rusty mountains, the great pale rhyolite column stands up to mark the place. It takes on different configurations and hues at different times of day and night. In some seasons the full moon rises directly behind it, and at all times it has a special affinity for the white radiance of moonlight. In another country and time it would have been a fane for Sîn or Phoebe. We do not know whether a divinity made it his dwelling and spoke from it to the Indian peoples, though we suppose that one did, or that spirits to be feared and propitiated lived about it. Certainly to white men it is cold and silent, beautiful to some, to others only eye-catching, a geographical marker, a reference point.

I am not talking about religious "belief," precisely. A modern man who is a believer will in some sense find God's presence in all his works. What I am talking about is the numinousness of a particular place, not the vague "religious" emotion with which we may respond to something beautiful or grand in nature. That is a pleasant and expansive feeling. Numinousness is to some degree mysterious, awful in the precise sense, whether it seems to bode well or ill. There is something besides belief which makes this feeling about ancient holy places still possible to a modern man. Even a Christian, an agnostic, or an atheist may feel, in the great mountain amphitheatre, the rumbling thunder, and the circling eagles, the numinousness of Delphi. Why? Because the place itself is invested with ancient myth and the enduring poetry which has celebrated it. Delphi has a poetic history, as Ireland has a poetic history. The Elephant's Tooth has none — none, at least, that we know. Therefore the white man's Oatman, the only one we can experience, has no history but the thinnest sort. It has little accumulation of human experience, none of mythology, nothing therefore to have been clothed in poetic vesture. To an old resident of the town, especially if he is a miner, this judgment may well seem not to be true; for his memory will be furnished with a rich history of his own and others' making. But I am speaking for anyone, relatively and in a larger sense — for all of us when we let our minds range over places and times, remote and at hand.

Besides, the comparison is not deprecatory. Places are only partly what they are by virtue of their history or lack of it. Therefore, to say so much is not to say that Oatman is not capable of moving us in other ways, or that it is without meaning, even profound meaning. What it has for us is its own severe beauty, a visible record of planetary upheaval. It has its special mark of that upheaval in the Elephant's Tooth, the day by day expected

feature of the landscape, yet the endless source of discovery
in the changing light of daybreak or sunset or moonlight. Oatman
has, for wonder, its desert contraries — the conserving toughness
of root, stem, and seed through long seasons of drought, the
renewing prodigality of fragile bloom at the touch of water in
a brief and occasional spring season. It has, too, for the long
reach of the imagination, its unobtrusive and mostly illegible
signs of earlier men who, like the desert lilies, the rock wrens,
and the jack rabbits, lived for countless generations on its scant
provisions and its seldom rains. But in our times Indian artifacts
do not flaunt themselves, as do the white man's rusting iron
and rotting boards, and belong to a past which can only be
imagined.

I have a special memory of Oatman. Once, when I was climbing with a companion up to the base of the Elephant's Tooth,
a great hawk rose from her eyrie on a cliff high above us. She
screamed at us as she hovered and circled. So Job's hawk and
eagle screamed on Mt. Seir in Edom:

> Doth the hawk fly by thy wisdom,
> And stretch her wings toward the south?
> Doth the eagle mount up at thy command,
> And make her nest on high?
> She dwelleth and abideth on the rock,
> Upon the crag of the rock, and the strong place,
> From thence she seeketh the prey,
> And her eyes behold afar off.

Inland Fog

Inland towns are not strangers to fog. I remember a Sunday in late January when a fog in Madison closed in everything. There was no color — white snow, white fog, gray trees vague in outline. The scene from my window on the Arboretum was done in silverpoint on a white ground.

As I walked to the end of my street, I met friends in a car, out on necessary business; they asked if they could take me anywhere, and where was I going anyhow on a day like this. "Just down to Lake Wingra," I said. "You won't see any lake," they said. But I knew what I should see. It would be the ghostly

grace of the willows retreating in definition along the shore,
the tangle of blonde sedges on the bank. I was going to visit
again, as one always revisits a favorite picture in a gallery, something seen before and loved.

This time there was something new — the unfloored pilings
of the boat piers going out into the ice of the frozen lake and
abruptly disappearing; the police boat pier with the planking
still on, warped upward with the pressure of the ice, also
abruptly ending nowhere. Ice and fog, the same color, became
one. But how far away was the limit of visibility? Twenty-five
yards? ten? five? One might calculate distance from the number
of pilings visible, but it was impossible to tell with the eyes
alone. With one's back turned to the shore, at least defined
by the willows and sedge, the look outwards towards the lake
was like the edge of a continent, the pilings like the foundations
of some abandoned camp on the shore of an Arctic island, or
on the Ross ice shelf in Antarctica. The very limitation of vision
impelled one to guess an immensity beyond — an unexplored
continent, a North or South Pole to be sought and reached,
its site unknown, the search fraught with danger.

The illusion could not be long sustained. The nearby noise
of melting droplets under the bank and around the pilings was
natural and not altogether disturbing of the illusion. The voices
of children, seemingly very near, but certainly across the lake,
were more so; for in implying a point beyond the ice they
imposed a boundary. The low roar of the traffic on the beltline
highway, still farther to the south, was more disturbing still.
We in the city were prisoners of its ring around us, of its wall
of sound, the more noticeable this day in the quiet of the fog
and in the illusion of remoteness it created.

For the circle of fog in which one walks should be the silentest
of places, the world shut out — a place to meditate in, but
not a fixed one. One moves in an envelope of space, shut in
but free, changing the boundaries at will. As one moves along

the usual daily route from where one lives to wherever one goes, one discovers the accidental features of it, one by one. Yet the mind is not engaged to these features as signs of a fixed place in the everyday way. To walk ten feet is to lose that lamp-post or that plum tree. When they come into view they are signs of nothing but themselves. One is therefore impelled to meditate on oneself as the center of a small universe, for though one can move it, and alter it somewhat by moving, one cannot break out of it. It is the mind which is freed. There are kinds of fog of which this sensation is not true. The green sulphurous London fog or the brown hydrocarbonated smog of an American city can be a suffocating prison. One feels clamped down under a heavy lid. But of these I am not speaking.

To a coast-dweller, like me, fog in Madison is always unexpected, and, I imagine, more welcome than to an inlander. To me it never seems a property of the place. I like it especially on Lake Mendota — not the blind, obliterating kind, but the lighter kind that softens outlines and changes perspectives, the kind in which the far shoreline is lost but Maple Bluff and Picnic Point are left, to stand like headlands between bay and an imagined open ocean beyond. To say this is not to wish that the lake be other than it is; it continually refreshes the spirit in the variety and unexpectedness of its moods and tones. But I happen to be especially moved by its misty aspect, when it appears unclosed, an opening to greater waters.

Why should I be? I hardly think the cause is a primordial memory of a time when we all came from the sea. Not that I am averse to the idea, an idea which, however, has always seemed to me more poetic than scientific, capable of much mysterious suggestion. A much simpler explanation is that I was brought up near the Pacific coast, of which fog was a property, not an accidental adjunct. There it might be at any time, enveloping the town, swathing the headlands, shutting out the sea, whose sibilant murmur became suddenly loud and declarative.

One gave it no particular attention unless it was dense enough to be hazardous to locomotion; it came and went, more frequently at some seasons than at others, but not unexpectedly at any time.

For anyone who has grown up on the sea-coast, fog has a weight of associations that cannot be easily shed. It belongs with the night sound of fog-horns on the bay, mournful, faintly yet pleasurably ominous; the startlingly near sound of unseen bell-buoys, impersonal, insistent; the measured roar and subsidence of the surf below the cliff road, the sound known more intimately and fearfully in every susurration than if the waves could be seen. Fog is a presence, not always there but at any time to be expected, and powerful when it comes. It is one of the old gods, whom one neither hates nor loves, but is respectful of, and wary of, and accommodates oneself to. One knows the fog, too, daily, in less numinous ways, for instance in the clamminess of underclothes left uncovered on a chair overnight, or in the damp chill of bed-linen which tightens the muscles and stiffens the body against sleep. I remember a night in February spent (near another coast) in a farmhouse on the Sussex downs — Cold Comfort Farm, I named it, after Stella Gibbons' novel. (You will recall that the farm of the Starkadder family was at Howling, Sussex.) The lady of the house had forgotten to put in my bed the comforting and necessary English hot water bottle. I lay stiff and shaking as the fog from the Channel sifted in through the casements and into the mattress and the blankets and me. Lying in a tight knot, I could not forget the cats in my sitting-room at dinner — huge, voracious, feral cats which closed in around my chair, intent with terrible eyes on every move of my hand. But this is a special case, a quintessential experience, to be cherished for an anecdote. I already knew the chilly winter sheets from my childhood on the southern California coast. They were taken for granted like corroding screens, mildewed books, sand in the bathtub, plugged holes in the salt-shakers.

On the Pacific coast the fog has a place to inhabit, to come from and go back to, and times to manifest itself; this it does dramatically, mostly in season, but sometimes not. The proper season is spring and summer. Then, in mid-afternoon the fog appears as a gray bank far out to sea on the western horizon. It seems to rise and approach at once, at first with wispy outriders, then with all of itself, swallowing sea and sunlight. In southern California this daily fog is most often flung as a night curtain between sky and land, not touching the land, but closing out the moon and the stars, and not pulled back to sea until the next mid-morning. Then it is known as a "high fog." If one breaks through the dull ceiling in an airplane, the upper side, in full sunlight, is like a dazzling hummocky snowfield, stretching out in an immense plain, broken by nearer hilltops and farther peaks, San Gorgonio and San Jacinto to the north, Palomar and Cuyamaca to the east, San Miguel to the southeast, and the mountains in Mexico, whose names one has never learned, off to the south. On the Peninsula, south of San Francisco, the afternoon fog rolls across the cliff-tops until it is stopped by the spine of the Coast Range. It fills the bowl of shore and mesa, and spills over the rim of the mountains, but its momentum has been checked. A dweller on the lee side watches the crest of it — a stilled breaker that holds its curve without smashing, yet runs long fingers through the torn edges of the skyline. Under the fog to windward, the artichokes grow and the sea-lions mate. But at the Golden Gate, the fog finds the gap and tumbles through into the bay. And at the city itself, where the barrier of hills is lower than on the Peninsula, the fog pours over, races down the streets on the lee slope, and almost in an instant has possessed the city with its dark chill.

I remember a drive with my mother, one spring afternoon just a few years ago, in Marin County beyond the Golden Gate. The road, towards the coast from the Muir Woods, was still a country road, winding, with steep gradients and short-radius turns. We came out on a view of the ocean below; here the road turned north and we could see it, now running near the coast, now away from it, up and down over the green hills. Unlike the southern California coast by then, or the Peninsula below San Francisco, the country looked rural and lightly peopled. The road invited us. Then we noticed the first patches of fog coming over the water. In a moment they were touching the edges of the land, joining and thickening, beginning to reach the rounded crowns of the hills. We were Californians; we turned and sped away.

Stevenson described these Pacific fogs in the Bay region in *The Silverado Squatters*, which was an account of his brief stay in 1880 in the Napa Valley and above it. From below, in the valley, the fog on spring mornings was to Stevenson poisonous: "fathoms on fathoms of gray sea vapour," hanging "thick and gray, and dark and dirty overhead." From above, looked down on from his summer refuge on the side of Mt. St. Helena and at a safe distance, the fog was a wonder. He describes its advance up the mountain, "the great Russian campaign for that season," one dramatic Sunday morning. At first, far below, it suggested the movement and surface of the sea, with a "smoky surf" beating about the foot of the precipices and pouring into all the coves of the mountains. The color of "that vast fog ocean" was something like what he had seen on the sea itself, among the Hebrides just about sundown. Yet the white of the sea was not so opaline, nor was there "that breathless, crystal stillness over all." When the fog rose high enough to threaten his retreat, the wind took it in a great silent torrent over the shoulder of the mountain into the next valley. Later, a veering of the wind sent it all quietly away.

The god of the Pacific fogs is not Mummu, that vague elemental spirit of watery land, who appears in mists over lake and marsh and the deltas of old rivers. That is the one who rises on Lake Mendota in clouds of cold steam on a morning in

December. This is a male god, a god of the sea, at war with land and sky, and in his appointed season daily reenacting his ancient enmity. Yet he brings to some creatures the gift of life. In southern California great beanfields used to cover the coastal mesas, for beans grow without irrigation if they are within reach of the sea fog. And one remembers that fog is the element of *Sequoia sempervirens.* On the northern California coast, from just above Crescent City down to Santa Cruz, the redwoods live in fog — in pockets in the hills, where it settles like water in tide-pools, or on steep mountainsides above the ocean, from which it swirls up about their trunks. In the dampness of the redwood groves, where sunlight, when it comes, is filtered through two hundred, three hundred feet, and more, of drooping fronds, young ferns uncoil and mountain sorrel spreads its white blossoms.

But it is not ocean fog we are talking about, is it? It is fog in Madison, and fog on Lake Mendota. The suggestion of the sea one may find in the misty shoreline of Mendota enriches the lake by hinting at an absence of limit, at something undefined beyond it, of an open ocean beyond a bay. Memory of past experience changes the very quality of the present. But the memory works in both directions. It also works to enrich the sea. One becomes sharply aware by their very absence of the things belonging to it — the smell of brine and seaweed, the stickiness of salt damp, the yodeling cries of willet and godwit, the slow, deliberate roar of the breakers, quite unlike the quick slap of fresh-water breakers, even of the size they sometimes attain on Lake Michigan. More especially, one discovers how intimate a part of oneself one's experience of the sea was.

It is because a change of place seems to stimulate the memory to work in this double way, of qualifying both present and past experience at the same time, that poets go to Europe to write about America. It is natural that one should discover one's country by going away from it. Learning comes in the recognition of sameness and difference. So Stevenson, in the sea fogs in the Napa Valley in California, learned something more of the sea off the coast of his native Scotland. If everything remains the same, we take all for granted and learn nothing; and complete difference is arresting or intriguing, but leaves us without a key to understanding. It is the sameness in difference that disturbs us, compels us to remember, to catch and hold something that might slip away, to think, to define. We always live in a context. We apprehend a thing in its surroundings, sensory or mental, physical or cultural. To move with our remembered experiences from a familiar context to an unfamiliar one jolts us into awareness, compels us to focus on the particulars of our surroundings, both old and new. It forces us, that is, to take things apart, but also invites us to put them together again with new meanings, or at least formerly unperceived meanings. It functions to release our minds from their everyday bonds and thereby free them for discovery of ourselves and what we are a part of.

Such an experience is something poets have told us about. It is like the night in the wood in *A Midsummer Night's Dream*, where the lovers, familiar to each other in certain ways when they were at home in Athens, now view each other through the effects of the love-juice in quite unfamiliar attitudes and relations. Through this topsy-turvy "night-rule" they learn to recognize and value the rule of day, in which relations are righted and in which fidelity in love has its place in the social order. The experience of discovery through a change of place is what happens in the Forest of Arden in *As You Like It* and on the island in *The Tempest*. In temporary retreat in the forest, Duke Senior

> Finds tongues in trees, books in the running brooks,
> Sermons in stones, and good in everything.

Nearly everyone in the play learns something about himself and where he belongs. On the magical island in the Mediterranean the same is true. *The Tempest* is about the discovery of who one is, and ought to be, as a human being.

Perhaps the reason the dense fog, the kind I spoke of at the beginning, the kind which shuts us in a circle not much beyond arm's reach, can be either so terrifying or so liberating, is that it so nearly destroys the sensory context we move about in every day. We are forced to be just ourselves, alone.

Bruegel
and the Pelican

One August evening I sat on the cliffs at La Jolla, watching the sea and the changing light. The sun had set. Although the golden path to the shore had gone, the water was still touched by the afterglow, and there was a rosy line at the fog bank along the horizon. Venus was a point of light in the west, Jupiter a lesser one in the southwest, near the pale crescent of the moon. The several lines of rollers, diminished from my height, were breaking in an orderly and unhurried way. The tide was beginning to come in and was lapping over the far edges of the tide-pool rocks.

It was a Saturday and little knots of people were sitting along the shore, some already lighting fires against the evening chill. Just below me a family was laying out a picnic supper. The smaller children, not yet gathered in, were running in and out of the water with their dog. Strollers, some in couples, were moving along the beach and out of sight. Signs of a busier world, though not intrusive, were about. Lights were coming on in clusters along the curve of the coast to the northwest — in the buildings of the Scripps Oceanographic Institute and on its pier, in the houses on the steep slope above it, at the town of Del Mar beyond it and of other little towns still farther on. A big plane going over and lowering altitude was headed south for the airport, out of sight on the shore of San Diego Bay. Close to shore, above the surf's edge and at about my eye level on the cliff, several small flocks of curlews went by, flying south in close formation with great speed and purpose. Unseen, the plants and animals of the pools on the rocks were quickening with the first drenchings of incoming water. A single brown pelican was still fishing, now skimming the tops of the waves just beyond the farthest breaker line, now plunging into a hollow between the crests.

All of these normal activities, appropriate to the doers' purposes, were geared to some schedule of time. The feeding and multiplying of the tide-pool creatures were governed by the moon's clock, daily and monthly; the pelican's fishing, by the sun's diurnal clock; the flights of the curlews, by both the diurnal and annual clocks of the sun and stars. The marine biologists and oceanographers, the crew and passengers on the plane, the people in the little towns, were following more complicated schedules, influenced by the astronomical clocks, but within that framework largely devised by themselves or by other human beings for them. The pilot, for instance, was flying his plane within a circumscribed pattern of place and time, one of thousands of similar intermeshed patterns made by men with the aid of computers; but his pattern was subject to interruption

or change, as Jupiter's appearance close to the new moon at
just that moment of time was not, at least within men's scale
of time. The passengers, held within the same pattern as the
pilot's for a few hours, expected to be, and were expected, on
the ground at Lindbergh Field at a certain hour and minute
of the day; from that moment, they would disperse, each on
his own separate and intended errand. Only the people on the
beach seemed free of time. To think so was an illusion. But
at least there was a lull, a slackening of the daily routine, a
loosening of the cords of the net, a beneficent idleness when
time ceased to press. The course was set; in a calm sea the
helmsman might safely take a turn about the deck. The slackening was the same for me. I sat in the still center, on a little
island of unconcern. To my eyes the scene was one of great
quietness and peace. The momentary plane and the curlews
only moved through it, not ruffling the calm.

That day in San Diego I had visited the Timken Gallery and
had looked for a long time at the elder Bruegel's "Parable of
the Sower." The style of the painting is suggested by the titles
it is given in various catalogues: "River Landscape with the Parable of the Sower," "The Estuary," "Paysage animé par la
Parabole du Semeur." As one might guess, it is typical of those
Bruegel compositions (like "The Hunters in the Snow," "The
Return of the Herd," "The Fall of Icarus") in which figures in
action appear prominently on a hill or rise of ground in the
left or right foreground, and in which other diminished figures
or other signs of human activity, such as farmhouses, churches,
towns, and ships, appear in a perspective landscape — the landscape a central plain or body of water with bordering mountains.

In the left foreground of our painting the only figure is the
sower on a hilltop. Behind him on the down slope is a farmstead,
and in the right foreground, on a lower slope of the hill, are
another farm and cottage. From these the eye moves across a
big house in a wood to a river, making a diagonal from the lower

right upwards towards the center. There it joins a wide bay or lake which nearly fills the whole central part of the picture and disappears at the top into a vague and misty distance. If the big body of water is meant to be the Sea of Galilee, the river must be the Jordan and flowing out of it rather than into it. In between the foreground and the flat left shore of river and lake the landscape is varied with woods, open farms, and a single church. On the far shore steep crags and jagged peaks make holds for castles and towers. On that side a city on level ground juts out into the open water, where boats and ships carry its commerce. A few high-flying birds appear against the sky in the distance; a nearer one, perhaps a crane, long-winged and long-necked, rises on the left near the tops of tall trees.

With his back to the farm buildings and the valley, the sower is walking forward, casting seed with his right hand and intent on his sowing. The bare and nearly level field, the rocky edge of it to the right where the hill falls off, and some thorny bushes ahead of him at the edge of the picture allow us to recall the seeds of the parable that fell, some by the wayside, some upon stony places, some among thorns, and other into good ground.

In the middle distance, on the far shore of the river, three boats are drawn up, and on the narrow beach, near one of these, there stands a knot of people towards which others are walking or running from both directions; two or three seem to be turning away. Not in the boat, as we should expect, but in the central cluster, a taller figure appears to be the one on whom the attention of the others is focused. One supposes this to be Jesus telling his listeners, hardly a great multitude, the first of his parables on the kingdom of heaven. But one cannot be sure which one is he. There is nothing to distinguish him, and from the viewer's standpoint the whole group is distant and very small in proportion to the sower in the foreground. Nothing striking directs one's attention to the group except the line of the river. The sower is not looking towards the gathering, could not at his level

be imagined to see it if he were. No more could Jesus be
imagined to perceive the sower. The pictorial emphasis, therefore, is not on the teacher, not even on the substance of the
thing taught, but only on the parable by which it is taught.
Used as we are to see episodes from the Gospels dramatically
represented, with Jesus as the usual compositional center (as
in the Italians and in Rembrandt), we may be startled by the
non-centered, non-dramatic representation of this one. The composition both arrested and puzzled me.

The method is like that of the more familiar "Fall of Icarus,"
in which all we are shown of Icarus' catastrophic experiment
with wings are his two small legs disappearing into the water
of a great bay. The only pictorial emphasis given them is in
the contrast of their light flesh color with the deep green water.
Again we have a spacious natural setting, with people in it going
about their daily tasks. The structural emphasis is on a big galleon
just offshore with its sails being taken in, and on three foreground
figures — a dominant plowman, nearest and largest; a shepherd
just below him, with his flock; and lower still, on the shore,
a fisherman. Not one of the three, and perhaps no one on the
ship, has noticed Icarus falling, not even the fisherman, though
he is close to the spot where the boy is drowning. The effect
is diminishing and ironic, more comic than tragic. The ambition
and daring of the youth, the originality of his father's invention,
even its failure, are nothing compared to the ongoing diurnal
and seasonal life of men doing necessary and unexciting things.

Are we to take the episode of Jesus' teaching by the Sea of
Galilee in the same ironic way? We hardly can. For we cannot
understand either painting without knowledge of the whole
story. The end of Icarus' adventure is in the picture, but Jesus,
in the depicted scene, is not halfway through his ministry, and
the ending of the story did not come even with the crucifixion.
We do not say, "This is how it ended," but "This is how it
began." We know that, as in the parable, some seeds of his

teaching "fell into good ground, and brought forth fruit, some a hundredfold, some sixtyfold, some thirtyfold"; we also know that the seeding and the harvest continue. The meaning implied in the painting by the compositional treatment of this particular episode is therefore complex, perhaps ambiguous, but hardly destructive. The primary focus on the acted-out parable puts the emphasis on the simplicity and homeliness of Jesus' teaching, hence on his own simplicity and, in one sense, commonness; therefore the greater wonder at the outcome — or perhaps the less, depending on how one looks at the matter. Again, the merely secondary focus on the scriptural event makes it seem just one among the diverse events of everyday life. If the busy world is unconscious of what is going on — for those hastening figures may suggest no more than the curiosity which always makes people run to join a crowd — the episode becomes, from one point of view, all the more significant and wonderful.

In the tissue of meanings suggested by the composition, with its greater and lesser focal points, there is another, even richer, implication. The mutual unawareness of each other of the figure speaking the parable and the figure enacting it is at first sight disconcerting, as if the congruence were merely accidental. But reflection suggests that this impression can hardly be Bruegel's intent. If Jesus cannot be presumed to see the actual sower on the hill, then we must assume he is teaching from his knowledge of the countryside and of people's seasonal labors. He would know, and his hearers would know, that this was the sowing season. The work would everywhere be going on and he would not need to point to a particular sower. The apparent independence of the two focal points in the composition is not therefore weakening but strengthening. It stresses the timelessness and universality of the teaching, its ever-renewed vitality. For the parable will have meaning so long as men sow grain and reap the harvest of it.

When later that day I sat on the cliff looking at my peaceful scene, I was struck by its resemblance to Bruegel's, not in its particulars but in its essential elements — a large natural setting, with nature just then in a temperate state, signs of an established society, people going about their normal affairs, even birds going about theirs. The only difference was the absence of any sign — seed falling into good ground, Elijah's cloud no bigger than a man's hand — of some pregnant happening, big with meaning for the future. Or if there were, I did not notice it.

But was that not precisely Bruegel's point? How should I recognize a sign if it were there? Even a potentially significant event if it were happening? I was myself part of the picture. To that man who had, since I began my reverie, taken a stand a little way off on the cliff, I must have been just a woman watching a pelican through binoculars, another figure in the scene *he* saw. How could I know whether the plane was not carrying one of its passengers to some urgent end which would affect all our lives? Whether a scientist behind that first cluster of lights up the coast was not at that moment in his observations arriving at some new knowledge about sea life which would, through use in the economy or in genetics, alter the future of the human race? Whether that meditative young man walking solitary on the beach was not plotting a revolution? Whether the child squealing at the antics of his wet puppy was not some future Freud or Marx, some Beethoven or Hitler or Ghandi? My awareness was superficial, limited to mere figures of people seen or imagined.

From another point of view I might seem less a part of the scene than the composer of it — not, of course, with Bruegel's complete freedom to choose its elements. For me the elements were given — the sea and sky, the lights along the coast, the people on the beach, the plane, the birds; and they were given only at a particular moment of time. Yet in this more limited way, by choosing, omitting, arranging, emphasizing, shaping a coherent statement, I was giving the scene form and meaning.

For no one else looking at the same actual things would the scene be quite the same as mine.

Still, I could not rightly detach myself from the scene either. I was part of it, and in an important way. The mood which prompted my reflections was not capricious or self-engendered. It was induced by a quality of the evening which I did not invent. I did not arbitrarily create in my mind harmonies which were not there. I was not alone in responding to the gentle evening. That couple who had sat hand in hand on a rock so long and quietly, the relaxed family, the child happy with the romping dog, others who came to stand silently on the cliff and look out to sea, the pelican prolonging his fishing, were all affected by it, consciously or not. They were drawn into its quietness.

As I watched, the light went out of the sky and off the water. The planets and the moon were becoming lustrous. The fires on the beach glowed with livelier red; the human figures were assumed into the darkness, except for momentary firelight on the faces. The coastline was now defined only by the lights and was lost where there were no habitations or roads. Another flight of curlews went south, this time close to the water and out at the near breaker line. The pelican stopped his fishing and flew with deliberate wingbeats to his nightly roost with fellows on a cliff-face up the coast. I arose, crossed the street into my apartment, and added my own point of light to the now unnumbered many up and down the shore.

Sometime in the night I awoke to hear, at high tide and loud in the still darkness, the rhythmic breathing of the sea — the crash and rumble of the breaking rollers, the hiss of the water as it rushed up the beach — ever varying, ever the same.

Notes

Notes

These notes are merely accessory, only for curious readers who may wish to follow a lead suggested by the text. Since to read the text with an eye on notes would be distracting, these are arranged by topic with reference to each essay.

SOMETHING ABOUT SWANS

The Explorers

On Scott's South Polar expedition, the zoologists E. A. Wilson and
Apsley Cherry-Garrard, with Lt. H. R. Bowers, made a remarkable
five-week journey on foot in the winter darkness of June–August, 1911,
from Scott's base camp at Cape Evans on McMurdo Sound to the
emperor penguin colony at Cape Crozier; see Scott's *Journals* for 25–27
June and 2 August 1911 (*Scott's Last Expedition: The Journals of Captain
Robert F. Scott*, arranged by Leonard Huxley, 2 vols. [New York:
Dodd, Mead, 1913], I, 229–30, 249–54); also Wilson's report and
Cherry-Garrard's diary of the journey (ibid., II, 1–52). Volume I has
been reissued in paperback by Beacon Press, Boston, 1957 (same
pagination). For the Kelley-Roosevelt-Field Museum expedition in Yun-
nan and Szechwan provinces of China in 1928–29, see *Trailing the Giant
Panda* by Theodore (the Younger) and Kermit Roosevelt (New York:
Scribner's, 1929). | *109*

The quotation from "Selborne" is from Chapter 14 in *Birds and Man* (London: Longmans, Green, 1901), pp. 304–5; and that from *Idle Days in Patagonia* (London: Chapman Hall, 1893) is in Chapter 4, pp. 54–55.

Audubon

The references to Audubon are to his journals and narratives as reprinted in *Audubon's America: The Narratives and Experiences of John James Audubon*, edited by Donald Culross Peattie (Boston: Houghton Mifflin, 1940), pp. 273–319 (on the Missouri River trip) and pp. 253–57 (on the Labrador trip). An account of his discovery on the latter trip (pp. 238–39) of the "Ruby-crowned Wren" (clearly the kinglet) anticipates in delight, if not in aesthetic judgment, my own experience with the kinglet: ". . . no person who has not heard it would believe that the song of this bird is louder, stronger, and far more melodious than that of the Canary bird. It sang for a long time ere it was shot, and perched on the tops of the tallest fir-trees removing from one to another as we approached. So strange, so beautiful was that song that I pronounced the musician . . . a new species of Warbler."

The Ouzel Nest

Murie's account of the nest, "Granite Creek — a Little Part of Jackson Hole," appeared in *Naturalist*, XII, no. 1 (Spring, 1961), 1–5; so also did his "testimony opposing construction of the dams" on the Upper Snake River, pp. 32–33, 36–39.

THE PLEASURES OF SECONDS

The Cuckoo

The translation from Hesiod's *Works and Days* (about 700 B.C.), lines 485–92, is by F. L. Lucas in *Greek Poetry for Everyman* (New York: Macmillan, 1951), p. 202. Aristotle's account of the cuckoo (*Historia Animalium*, 563b14 ff., and the possibly spurious 618a8 ff.) makes it safe to assume that the Greek κόκκυξ (kókkux) is the same as the English bird of the same name — not in all cases a safe assumption; think of the English and American robins! See also D'Arcy Wentworth Thompson, *A Glossary of Greek Birds*, new ed. (London: Humphrey Milford, 1936).

The three referring to wild geese are from *A Further Selection from the Three Hundred Poems of the T'ang Dynasty*, translated by Soame Jenyns (London: John Murray, 1944), pp. 64, 92, and 66, respectively. The one on the agricultural year is from *The Book of Songs*, translated by Arthur Waley (Boston: Houghton Mifflin, 1937), no. 159, pp. 164–67.

LISTENING

Bird Song

Everyone knows Chaucer's early morning bird song in the Prologue to *The Canterbury Tales.* An anonymous fifteenth-century poet turned the spring morning chorus into the service of matins, sung on May Day to honor the God of Love; when the lark arose, the nightingale, who had not been able to sleep, began the service with *Domine labia* ("My lippes open, lord of love, I crie") and all the others sang their parts in turn — the eagle, the falcon, the goldfinch, the merle, the robin redbreast, the turtle dove, the throstle cock, and others (from "The Court of Love," first published in John Stow's edition of Chaucer, 1561; for edited text, see Wm. Skeat's edition of Chaucer's *Works* [Oxford: Press, 1894–97] VII, 446–47).

The references to Hudson are to Chapter 3, "Bird Music in South America" (quotation, pp. 149–50) and Chapter 13, "The Plains of Patagonia" (especially pp. 215–16), in *Idle Days in Patagonia* (New York: Appleton, 1893).

Eiseley

Both of the quotations from Eiseley are in Chapter 3, "The Hidden Teacher," in *The Unexpected Universe* (New York: Harcourt Brace and World, 1964), pp. 53–55; but see the whole book, and also *The Immense Journey, passim* (New York: Random House, [1957]).

Films of "Romeo and Juliet"

The Zeffirelli film opened in New York on 8 October 1968; see *New York Times Film Reviews*, 9 October 1968; for a sympathetic review of the director's full exploitation of his visual medium, see Albert R. Cirillo, "The Art of Franco Zeffirelli and Shakespeare's *Romeo and Juliet*," *TriQuarterly*, no. 16 (Fall, 1969), 69–93.

Castellani's film opened in New York on 21 December 1954; see *New York Times Film Reviews*, 22 December 1954; for a defense of it, see Paul A. Jorgensen, "Castellani's *Romeo and Juliet:* Intention and Response," *Quarterly of Film, Radio, and Television*, X (1955), 1–10.

A SOLEMNITY

The Spanish Explorations and California Place Names
For accounts of the early coastal explorations, with logs, charts, and journals, see Henry R. Wagner, *Spanish Voyages to the Coast of America in the Sixteenth Century* (San Francisco: Calif. Historical Society, 1929): for Cabrillo, Chapter 4 (p. 85 on "San Miguel," bestowed on what is now San Diego Bay on 29 September, the day after its first discovery in 1542); for Vizcaino, Chapters 10, 11 (pp. 231–32 and n. 125 on the second naming of "San Diego").

The standard account of the two land expeditions of Anza in 1774 and 1775–76 is by Herbert E. Bolton in his *Anza's California Expeditions* (Berkeley: Univ. Calif. Press, 1930), vol. I; the translated diaries of Anza and his companions are in volumes II–IV. For Father Crespi's diary, see Bolton's translation in *Fray Juan Crespi* (Berkeley: Univ. Calif. Press, 1927); for Father Garcés' diary of his trip alone, see Elliott Coues' translation, *On the Trail of a Spanish Pioneer* (New York: Harper, 1900), I, 241–48, or John Galvin's more recent one, *A Record of Travels in Arizona and California, 1775–1776* (San Francisco: J. Howell, 1965).

On the names of San Jacinto and San Gorgonio Mountains, see Erwin R. Gudde, *California Place Names*, 3rd ed., revised (Berkeley: Univ. Calif. Press, 1969), p. 286; also Phil Townsend Hanna, *The Dictionary of California Land Names*, revised ed. (Los Angeles: Automobile Club of Southern Calif., 1951), pp. xii–xiii, 275. Hanna thinks unlikely the naming of the peaks from the ranches. See Gudde also under "Crespi," p. 381.

Saints' Lives
The most delightful way to become acquainted with Jacobus de Voragine's great popular collection, the *Legenda Aurea* (Genoa, ca. 1170), is in Wm. Caxton's English version (Westminster, ca. 1483); it may be found in The Temple Classics, ed. F. S. Ellis (London: Dent,

1900), 7 vols. For Saint Gorgonius of Nicomedia, see Ellis' edition,
V, 119 (feast day, September 9); for the Saint Hyacinth who was one
of the companions of Saint Eugenia, V, 120–25 (September 11).

I have consulted the two standard, many-volume lives of the saints
in both their early and their later revised versions: Alban Butler's *Lives
of the Saints* and Sabine Baring-Gould's *Lives of the Saints*; also the
one-volume *Book of Saints*, compiled by the Benedictine Monks of
St. Augustine's Abbey, Ramsgate. The newer, revised editions are
usually less full and less interesting, with doubtful and legendary matter
pruned away. Herbert Thurston's *Dictionary of Saints* (London: Burns,
Oates, and Washbourne, 1938) is designed as an index to his revised
edition of Butler (London: Burns, Oates, and Washbourne, 1926–38).

For a full list of the eight Saints Hyacinth, consult the index to *The
Book of Saints*, first ed. (London: H. and C. Black, 1921); all but
Saint Hyacinth of Poland (August 17, formerly 16) are early Roman
martyrs, some under Trajan, most of unknown date. The fullest accounts
of "the Apostle of Poland," including lively legends as well as facts,
are in Butler's old (first compiled in 1756–59) *Lives of the Fathers,
Martyrs, and Other Principal Saints* (I have seen the Dublin edition
of 1845, VIII, 185–91) and in Baring-Gould, revised ed. (London:
Nimmo, 1897–98), IX, 151–54. Hanna (*Dictionary of California Land
Names*, p. 275) is less positive than Gudde (*California Place Names*,
p. 286) that he is the San Jacinto of the mountain.

Baring-Gould's observations on the life of Saint Eugenia are in his
volume X, pp. 166, 168.

The Indians

For convenience I use the still familiar Spanish names given the Indians
according to the missions to which they were attached. Their own tribal
names and linguistic affinities are anthropological matters in which I
have no competence; for guidance consult especially A. L. Kroeber,
Handbook of the Indians of California (Smithsonian Institution, Bureau
of American Ethnology, Bulletin 78 [Washington, D.C.: Government
Printing Office, 1925]). For "Takwish," the evil spirit on San Jacinto,
see Gudde, p. 329, under "Tahquitz," the name now borne by the
lesser peak of San Jacinto Mountain; Kroeber, "California Place Names
of Indian Origin," *University of California Publications in American*

114 Anthropology and Ethnography, XII, no. 2 (June 15, 1916), 60–61; and Lucile Hooper, "The Cahuilla Indians," *University of California Publications in American Anthropology and Ethnography*, XVI, no. 6 (April 10, 1920), 364–65.

The Desert
Informative books on the Mojave and Colorado Deserts are three by Edmund C. Jaeger, for many years a zoologist at Riverside Junior College (now the University of California, Riverside): *The California Deserts*, 2nd ed., revised (Stanford, Calif.: Stanford Univ. Press, 1938), on geology, physiography, weather, flora, and fauna; *Our Desert Neighbors* (Stanford, 1950), on animals, birds, and reptiles; *Desert Wildflowers*, revised ed. (Stanford, 1941), a complete reference book, with descriptions and sketches of 764 plants. (My references to desert plants are to the latter book, which I follow in the use both of common and of scientific names.)

The Bigelow Cholla
This cactus (*Opuntia Bigelovii*) is also called "teddy-bear" cholla (pronounced "choya") from its fuzzy appearance, or "jumping" cholla from the alacrity with which the small, egg-like joints, close-set with barbed spines, detach themselves from the parent plant and attach themselves to the flesh of the passerby. They are the cruelest of the several varieties of cholla, and so far as I am concerned the cruelest of all the cactuses. They propagate rapidly just by dropping their ball-shaped joints, which soon take root and spread in dense stands.

The White Pelicans
On their nesting site in Pyramid Lake, see Nell Murbarger, "The Birds of Anaho," *Natural History*, June, 1956, pp. 300–305; the fish in Pyramid Lake, a fresh-water lake, were evidently even then insufficient for the pelicans. The lake is now so rapidly shrinking from drainage for irrigation that Anaho Island may soon be a peninsula — and then an end to the pelicans.

THE DESERT SPARROW

The Sparrow
"Desert sparrow" is still the common local name of *Amphispiza bilineata*, or black-throated sparrow. An account of it and of other spar-

rows resident in the desert may be found in Jaeger's *Our Desert*
Neighbors (see note to "A Solemnity"), pp. 100–104.

The Plants

Since those I have referred to may be easily located in Jaeger's *Desert Wildflowers*, I comment here only on the few for which the common names may be misleading or not informing. The desert sunflower (*Geraea canescens*) is not a true sunflower or *Helianthus* and is only six inches to two feet tall, but it makes a splendid show wherever it grows in abundance. The famous sand-verbena of the dunes (*Abronia villosa*) is not a verbena but a four-o'-clock. Of the "belly-flowers," purple mat (*Nama demissum*) belongs to the waterleaf family; frost-mat (*Achyronychia Cooperi*) to the pink family; desert calico (*Gilia Matthewsii*) to the phlox family. The sand blazing star (*Mentzelia involucrata*), of the loasa family, is only one of a number of handsome members of the genus, all in shades of cream or yellow, and is without relation in color, form, or family to the midwestern purplish blazing stars, or gayfeathers (*Liatris*), of the daisy family. The unusual ghost-flower (*Mohavea confertiflora*) belongs to the figwort family.

A POSTCARD FROM DELPHI

Geology and Mining History

The Black Mountains form a highly complex geological and mineralogical region, of which no simple description can be made. For an account, consult F. S. Schrader, *Mineral Deposits in the Cerbat Range, Black Mountains, and Grand Wash Cliffs, Mohave County, Arizona*, Department of the Interior, U.S. Geological Survey, Bulletin 397 (Washington, D.C.: Government Printing Offiice, 1909), especially pp. 27–42. The Elephant's Tooth is an exposed part of a rhyolite dike; it is buff, pinkish, or yellowish, depending on the light.

Gold in the region was discovered in the early sixties; the railroad came in in 1882 and stimulated mining (Schrader, pp. 43–45, 181, 192–99). But the period of great production at Gold Road and at Oatman did not begin until after the turn of the century.

The Hawk

The nesting hawk on the cliff near the Elephant's Tooth appeared to be a Swainson's hawk and the rather high-pitched cries seemed to be a Swainson's, but these hawks may not be commonly in the region, as western redtails are; the intense light in the sky made distinction of markings difficult.

Irish Art

On the continuity of design between ancient and Celtic art, consult Françoise Henry, *Irish Art in the Early Christian Period to A.D. 800,* 3rd ed. (London: Methuen, 1965), p. 204; but see the whole book, especially Chapters 1 and 8. Cf. also the examples of pagan and Christian art in the National Museum, Dublin.

The Indians

On the Patayan culture (formerly called Yuman) of the people of this region, see H. M. Wormington, *Prehistoric Indians of the Southwest* (Denver Museum of Natural History, Popular Series No. 7, 3rd ed., 1956), chap. 7. Partly because of the obliteration of signs by the frequent flooding of the Colorado in earlier times, much less is known of these people than of the Anasazi of the Four Corners region (probably ancestors of the Pueblo Indians) and the Hohokam of central and southern Arizona (probably ancestors of the Pima and Papago Indians).

London Bridge

The relatively modern nineteenth-century structure, which has now been "relocated at a cost of 8.4 million," is, of course, not the old bridge of the nursery rhyme. Early in 1970 we were all invited by McCulloch Properties, Inc., through newspaper advertisements and direct-mail brochures, to "fly to the wonderful small world of Lake Havasu City, Arizona," without cost, and leave our "Big City" problems behind us. Now, Lake Havasu City is already a sizeable community, spread over several square miles, and is in the way of fulfilling the Honorable Paul J. Fannin's dream of it as "a light-industry center, a sportsman's mecca, a vacation resort that will provide service to millions of visitors in the years to come, and a retirement haven," with "a projected population of 60,000 residents" (from his speech in the Senate, 21 October 1965; reprinted from the *Congressional Record,* 89th Congress, First Session). After a reading of Senator Fannin's eloquent speech on the future of this "instant city" (his phrase), this essay of mine seems to me as archaic as a prehistoric Yuman's geometric symbols carved into the desert varnish.

San Francisco Fog
Perhaps it was the sea fog which kept the entrance to San Francisco Bay so long hidden from the eyes of explorers (beginning with Cabrillo in 1542) probing the coast for harbors for New Spain. It was not certainly discovered until 1769, and then by Portolá from the land side. Anza, founding a presidio and a mission on the bay in 1776, commented on the almost nightly fogs. For the explorations by sea and land, see references in note to "A Solemnity"; also, for the uncertainties of Drake's anchorage in 1579, whether San Francisco Bay or another, Henry R. Wagner's *Sir Francis Drake's Voyage around the World* (San Francisco: J. Howell, 1926).

Mummu
Mummu is one of the three primordial beings of the watery chaos in the Mesopotamian creation epic, *Enûma elish* (Akkadian). Apsu, the husband, is the primeval sweet-water ocean, the water later welling up from underground; Tiamat, the wife, is the salt-water ocean; Mummu, not defined, appears to be the mist rising from the two bodies of water and lying over them. See Alexander Heidel, *The Babylonian Genesis*, 2nd ed. (Chicago: Univ. Chicago Press, 1951), pp. 3, 18, 57; also Thorkild Jacobsen, "Mesopotamia," in *The Intellectual Adventure of Ancient Man* (Chicago: Univ. Chicago Press, 1946), p. 170.

BRUEGEL AND THE PELICAN

The Paintings
"The Parable of the Sower" is a little-known painting of Bruegel's (signed and dated 1557), in a poor state of preservation and not often reproduced. It was found in Antwerp only in 1931, was on loan for some time to the National Gallery of Art in Washington, D.C., and was acquired by the San Diego Fine Arts Gallery in 1965. A reproduction of it, not in color, appears in the Phaidon Press *Bruegel: The Paintings, Complete Edition* (London, 1955; revised ed., 1966), plate 5 and note (p. 190); also in *Bruegel* (Brussels: Arcade, 1969), plates 13 (detail of Jesus addressing the multitude) and 14, Catalogue no. 5 (see p. 81), where it is erroneously described as being still on loan to the National Gallery.

The reference usually given for the parable is to Matthew 13:3–8; but it appears in nearly the same form in Mark 4:3–8 and Luke 8:5–8. In all three, Jesus speaks from the boat. I have to rely on my notes for the figure in the painting I took to be Jesus and for the absence of one in the boat. The reproductions are not large enough to settle the matter.

"The Fall of Icarus" exists in two versions, the one in the D. M. van Buuren Collection (Brussels and New York), with a large winged figure in the sky, as if before the fall, and the other, without the winged figure, in the Brussels Musées Royeaux des Beaux-Arts. This is the one most often reproduced and the one my comments are based on. For the question of authenticity, see the Phaidon Press *Bruegel*, plates 3 and 3a and note (pp. 189–90), or the Arcade *Bruegel*, plates 1–8 (Catalogue no. 3, p. 81).

DESIGNED BY SYLVIA SOLOCHEK WALTERS

MANUFACTURED BY THE NORTH CENTRAL PUBLISHING CO., ST. PAUL, MINNESOTA

TEXT LINES ARE SET IN CALEDONIA, DISPLAY LINES

IN GARAMONT AND CALEDONIA

Library of Congress Cataloging in Publication Data
Doran, Madeleine, 1905–
Something about swans.
Includes bibliographical references.
CONTENTS:
Something about swans. — The pleasures of seconds. — Listening. [etc.]
1. Doran, Madeleine, 1905–   I. Title.
PS3507.073225Z52   814'.5'2   73-2042
ISBN 0-299-06170-1